Household Tips

Household Tips

Over 1000 fix-its for your home

Judith Millidge

PRC

Produced in 2004 by
PRC Publishing Limited
The Chrysalis Building
Bramley Road, London W10 6SP

An imprint of **Chrysalis** Books Group

ISBN 1 85648 723 7

Printed and bound in Malaysia

Contents

INTRODUCTION

"I must frankly own, that if I had known, beforehand, that this book would have cost me the labour which it has, I should never have been courageous enough to commence it. What moved me, in the first instance, to attempt a work like this, was the discomfort and suffering which I had seen brought upon men and women by household mismanagement."

Isabella Beeton THE BOOK OF HOUSEHOLD MANAGEMENT

Mrs Beeton's classic work, published in 1861, embraced every aspect of household management from hiring servants, to feeding infants, from precise etiquette in all areas of life, to listing hundreds of nourishing recipes for every occasion. Sadly, the scope of this book is slightly less wide-ranging, but, in this time-hungry age, it will be equally useful (and it's much shorter than Mrs Beeton's redoubtable volume). It is not meant to be an intensive "how-to" guide; instead it is a collection of hints and tips designed to make tedious and necessary household jobs quicker, easier, and sometimes, cheaper. So there are no long explanations of exactly how to start certain projects like painting and decorating—we have assumed that you have a basic knowledge of the task in hand—and merely seek to pass on a few hints that might make the job more straightforward. When tackling any job, it is vital to be aware of safety and one's own limitations. There are also circumstances when professional help is not only vital, but a legal requirement, so please consider that before embarking on any project.

The tips have been compiled from a wide variety of sources and cover everything from compost heaps to computers. Energy saving advice is included, but so are short-cuts for busy people: remember that timesaving tips are not always the cheapest or "greenest" solution.

One of the most important and valuable household tips has been passed on, as all the best ones are, by my mother: get staff. There is nothing more depressing than returning from a hard day's work to find a house in the state that you abandoned it in when you left in a rush in the morning. On the other hand, returning to clean kitchen surfaces and ordered rooms is an enormous pleasure. Paying for the expertise of skilled craftsmen, gardeners, cleaners, and others is often a worthwhile investment if you can afford it.

In realistic terms, paying for domestic help is simply not an option for many people, and the way forward for domestic order is simply organization and a bit of knowledge. This book will help provide it.

A Clean House

Cleaning—can't live with it, can't live without it. No one really enjoys cleaning (or I've yet to meet anyone who does), but it is a necessary part of maintaining your house in good order and a vital part of keeping you and your family in good health. And you might just get a sneaking feeling of satisfaction while contemplating what is probably a temporarily tidy house. The writer and aesthete Quentin Crisp famously remarked that "There is no need to do any housework at all. After the first four years the dirt doesn't get any worse." Most of us, however, are less resilient in the face of accumulating grime. Furthermore, keeping a house and our possessions clean is one way of preserving them and ensuring that they remain useful as long as possible. It really makes no sense to neglect the things we own—it's simply a waste of hard-earned cash!

If you really are short of time, just tidy a room: put everything away in its correct place, clear up cups and mugs, throw out old flowers, and empty the bin/garbage can. The room will instantly look much better.

Sew up the bottom of an old apron to make a big pocket. Wear it as you go round the house, and use it to collect any stray items before returning them to their rightful places.

PLANNING &
PREPARATION

One of the first cleaning tips is to face up to your responsibilities. Decide what needs to be done every week and if necessary draw up a timetable, allocating one or two tasks to every day. You can blitz the whole house in one go if you'd rather, but little and often may fit in better with your schedule.

Aim to wipe down your bathroom sink and clean the toilet every day. Similarly, the kitchen must be kept clean, so wipe down surfaces every day and clear the washing-up.

Vacuuming and dusting are weekly jobs, so set aside a regular time for tackling the living rooms and bedrooms.

☞ Get organized.

☞ Get the right equipment.

☞ Make a rota or timetable.

☞ Tackle one or two jobs every day.

☞ Use labor-saving items such as disinfectant wipes and
   impregnated disposable dusters to save time. (They won't
   save you money, however!)

☞ Empty your vacuum cleaner regularly—there's nothing worse
   than discovering a burst bag just when you're in a hurry to
   clean up.

☞ Enlist the help of other household members.

If you are a "morning person," that is you function more efficiently early
in the day, try to get a few chores done before you go to work. That way,
you won't be faced with tedious jobs when you arrive home tired after
a day at work. And it's always far more pleasant to find a reasonably
ordered home on your return. You can make your life easier by doing the
following:

☞ Clear up glasses, snack wrappers, newspapers, etc from
   your living room before retiring for the night.

☞ Clear up breakfast items before you leave in the morning.

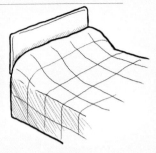

☞ Make the bed.

☞ Insist to other members of the family
that these are the minimum standards
expected of everyone!

EQUIPMENT

The next thing is to prepare your armory to tackle the various jobs—preparation is half the battle here. Make sure you have supplies of washing-up liquid or liquid soap for everyday washing up, and the necessary cleaning products for your dishwasher if you have one. There are hundreds of cleaning products on the market, but you really do not need a huge variety. One anti-bacterial or bleach-based cream, gel or spray for the kitchen, another for the bathroom, household bleach for the toilets, aerosol polish for light dusting, and wax for treating wooden pieces once a month should suffice. You can add preparations for windows, hard floors, silver, brass, and so on if you wish.

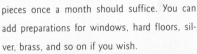

Make sure you have suitable hardware—a vacuum cleaner, a bucket, mop, rubber gloves, a mildly abrasive sponge for ceramic bathroom surfaces, a washing–up brush for crockery, and an abrasive pad for stained items. A broom and a dustpan and brush are also useful. Two brushes are better—one with stiff bristles and one with softer ones. Dusters are also vital. You can buy disposable cloths, or cut up old bits of cotton, whichever you prefer. Old pajamas or t-shirts are especially good!

Your cleaning kit will also need regular maintenance if it is to remain effective. When you buy a vacuum cleaner, make sure it is the right height for you and that you can carry it comfortably, particularly if you live in a house with stairs. If you have pets or suffer from respiratory problems, consider getting one with extra filters to deal with pet hairs and allergy-inducing microdust.

Wash brooms and brushes occasionally in a solution of liquid soap, then rinse in warm water, followed by cold salty water that will stiffen the bristles. Leave them to dry with the bristles upright—either hang them by their handles or prop them up against a bucket.

Take it from the top

If you do decide to clean the whole house in one go, start from the top
and work down—in this way you work with gravity not against it. Dust
dislodged from the upper storeys will filter downstairs, so if
you start on the bottom, you may find you need
to repeat the dusting after you've done the
top floor!

The same applies to cleaning stairs: always
begin the vacuuming at the top if possible, because dust and dirt will
almost certainly be knocked down the stairs as you vacuum.

Make sure that you leave the bathroom until last in case you need to
visit it for fresh water for your cleaning bucket.

Vacuum or sweep a room first, as this generally raises dust, and then
dust the surfaces.

Make good use of the hose attachments on the vacuum cleaner as they
can save a lot of time and effort in cleaning high spots, hard-to-reach
corners, and tricky objects such as curtains, blinds, and lamp shades.

DUSTING

Dampen your duster slightly before you begin, as dust adheres to a damp cloth far more effectively.

Take a plastic sack with you as you work your way around the house to empty wastepaper baskets; this will save you running to and fro to the main bin/garbage can.

Remove dust from large-leafed house plants by rubbing the leaves with the inside of a banana skin. This also nourishes and shines the leaves really well.

Computer keyboards quickly become dusty or clogged with small crumbs and particles of skin. Instead of using a duster, use the small brush attachment of your vacuum cleaner to remove everything. Do the same to the vents on the back of the TV set. Never spray aerosol cleaners or water around electrical items such as the TV, VCR, or DVD player.

Vacuuming

Always begin in the corner of the room farthest from the door and work your way out. In this way, you will avoid traipsing in more dust from your feet or from the vacuum cleaner.

Vacuum the clear areas of floor first, then move the furniture to vacuum underneath.

Use the brush attachments for awkward corners and skirting boards.

Traditional cleaning preparations

You can avoid using commercial preparations to clean your house by substituting cleaners made from less toxic substances. If you suffer from allergies or sensitivity to modern chemical cleaning products, try using some of the items below. They clean just as well as commercial preparations at a fraction of the cost. And even if you prefer to stick with tried and tested brands, these items can be used in an emergency.

WHITE WINE VINEGAR will remove limescale, clean windows and neutralize some odors. It is acidic, so use with caution on plated and metal surfaces.

LEMON JUICE is a milder acidic cleaner and a natural bleaching agent. Fresh lemon juice and the concentrated bottled form are equally effective. Mix three parts salt to one part lemon juice for a copper and brass cleaning solution.

CLUB SODA will disperse red wine and coffee stains.

TOILET SOAP will last longer if kept in the airing cupboard and will remove a great many marks from upholstery and fabrics.

BAKING SODA (bicarbonate of soda) will act as a mild abrasive to remove dirt and grease. It can be used on sinks, stoves, and basins in the same way as a powdered scourer and will shine stainless steel really well. As it is a mild alkaline substance, it will help remove acidic stains, such as those caused by fruit juice. It is also a natural deodorizer, and can be sprinkled on upholstery to dispel pet odors, on musty mattresses, or on upholstery in cars.

WASHING SODA CRYSTALS can be mixed with baking soda to make a stronger abrasive cleaner. They cut through grease and are excellent for washing down kitchen surfaces. They are also useful as a drain cleaner, and can be used neat or with a small amount of hot water added.

CLEANING WINDOWS & MIRRORS

Achieving a smear-free window is a sign that you have reached domestic nirvana, but it is not easy. Consequently, there are many dozens of hints and tips to choose from; try a few and see what works best for you.

The first is to purchase a proprietary cleaner which promises smear-free glass. These are generally reasonably efficient and are certainly a quick way of cleaning your windows.

Always clean windows on dull days. If it is sunny, the window may dry too quickly leaving tell-tale smears.

One trusty tip is to roll old newspapers into a pad and use them to clean windows. Apparently the acid in the ink helps to remove grease and grime. This is probably the cheapest option and you certainly have nothing to lose by trying it.

To remove paint splashes or bird droppings from windows, soak a rag in hot vinegar and rub over the marks. You may need to polish the windows once the marks have been removed.

After you have washed windows with soapy water, sprinkle a cloth with vinegar and rub the windows to remove soap film. Polish the windows with a dry, lint-free cloth for a really good shine.

Use horizontal strokes on the interior and vertical on the exterior—that way, if you have smears, you'll know which side of the pane of glass needs attention.

KITCHENS

Kitchens are the center of many homes, and may be occupied pretty much all the time as the family flits through, lingers for a coffee, enjoys their supper, or prepares meals. It can quickly become cluttered with bags, homework, letters, toys, and anything else that is abandoned as people pass through. And this is in addition to the considerable array of food, crockery, pots and pans, gadgets, and all the other items that are already stored there.

It can be difficult to maintain a tidy kitchen, but stamp down hard on serial offenders who leave their clutter lying around. Issue a deadline and confiscate or even throw away items that are not collected after a certain time. Discourage pets from walking on kitchen work surfaces, and keep them clear.

- Store gadgets that are rarely used in a cupboard.
- Store food as soon as you return from the supermarket, especially chilled or frozen items.
- Put away foodstuffs and tools when you have finished preparing meals.
- If your washing machine is in the kitchen, do not sort laundry on work surfaces and when you empty the

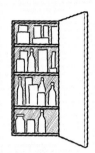

machine, try to remove the clothes and dry them elsewhere.

☞ Make sure that there is nothing left within reach of small children or pets, such as trailing electric flexes, knives, or anything else that may present a hazard.

☞ Remove dirty pans, utensils and crockery to the sink and stack it prior to washing up.

Kitchen hygiene

Once the clutter has been cleared, concentrate on kitchen hygiene.

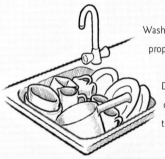

Wash kitchen surfaces regularly with hot water and a proprietary cleaner.

Do not use your washing-up cloths for wiping down kitchen surfaces, because this will merely transfer bacteria. Kitchen sponges harbor millions of germs and microbes and should be changed regularly—at least once a week; some hygienists advocate every day! If you purchase several cotton weave dishcloths, there will be enough to wash them daily, either with a white wash, or in the dishwasher when you clean the crockery.

Change your tea towels every couple of days, too. Damp towels harbor germs which will be transferred to every item you wipe.

Use very hot water for washing up as it will kill bacteria. Tip out murky or cool water as bacteria will flourish in these conditions.

Clear up pet food bowls after every meal as they will attract flies, bugs, and germs.

The same is true of crockery, pots, and pans that have been used to prepare meals for the resident humans. Even if you don't want to wash them up immediately, rinse them and stack them in the sink.

Always wash your hands in hot soapy water before you begin to prepare a meal. Wash them again when you have handled raw meat and dry them thoroughly on kitchen paper or a hand towel. Do not use your tea towels for anything other than drying the washing-up.

Use at least two chopping boards, and try to dedicate one to meat preparation. It is all too easy to transfer the microbes in raw meat to your hands and from there to your stomach, resulting in food poisoning.

POTS & PANS

We generally expect a lot from our cookware, dousing it in sticky substances and subjecting it to a daily furnace of heat. In order to preserve pans as long as possible, make sure you look after them. When buying cookware, buy the best you can afford. This is an area in which you really do get what you pay for. If you can stretch to brands with a "lifetime guarantee," it is probably worth the extra money and will potentially save you from nasty accidents when handles split or lids fall apart. Consider buying items intended for professional chefs as they are usually excellent quality and long-lasting.

When cleaning cookware, always try to wash items as soon as possible after use. Baked-on residues and stains get worse, not better with the passage of time. Try to soak the item after use, even if you don't wash it immediately.

If a pan has become burnt, clean it by simmering some onion skins in it for an hour (and make sure that it does not boil dry). Leave it to cool overnight and in the morning the blackened particles should simply slide away.

Another method of removing burnt residues is to sprinkle baking soda in the pan, then moisten it very slightly with water, Leave it to stand for several hours or overnight and then rinse off everything, baking soda, burnt bits, and all. You may need to use a spatula or wooden spoon to remove the really tough bits.

Salt removes burns and scorch marks from pie dishes, stains from china, and egg stains from cutlery.

Use a cleaning method that is appropriate to the pan. So do not use an abrasive pad with non-stick or teflon items, for example, or the non-stick finish will quickly disappear.

If your non-stick frying pan has become discolored, soak it overnight in a mild solution of household bleach, then rinse well.

If ageing baking trays or cake tins begin to go a little rusty at the corners, try scouring them with a raw potato that has been dipped in a proprietary cleaning powder.

Heavy-bottomed enamel saucepans need special treatment, especially when new, so always follow the manufacturer's instructions before using them for the first time.

If you do end up with a burnt enamel pan, sprinkle in a mixture of one tablespoon of salt and two tablespoons of lemon juice. Leave for a half hour, then rub gently with a fine wire scrubber or steel wool to remove the burnt particles.

Improve the appearance of copper-bottomed pans by smearing cold baked beans on the copper and leaving for a couple of hours. Rinse off the beans to reveal shiny copper which is almost as good as new.

Before broiling or grilling food, line the pan with foil. This not only increases the efficiency of the heat, but it also makes cleaning much quicker; the fat-encrusted foil can simply be thrown away, making cleaning the pan much easier.

If you spill fat on the floor or kitchen surface, pour on a little cold water immediately. This will set the fat, enabling you to scrape off the worst of it. Remove the remainder with hot soapy water.

Cleaning barbecue equipment is usually a messy job, but if you remember to rub a cake of soap over the bottom of pans before use, the smoke stains will disappear really easily when washed.

If your wooden bread board or chopping board has become discolored, give it a daily scrub with salt water. Scrub in the direction of the grain and then rub a cut lemon over the wood to bleach it. Dry the board outdoors, if possible, as ultraviolet light naturally disinfects the wood.

Treat roasting tins to a soak in biological washing power and warm water. Leave to soak for an hour or so, then rinse out. If the stains are particularly bad, heat the solution in the tin on the hob for about ten minutes, then wash as normal.

Ovens

Ovens receive a fair bit of punishment, but like almost everything else in the kitchen, it is best to clean them regularly and often to avoid a build-up of grease and grime, which is not only unsightly, but also incredibly unhygienic. Like any machine, an oven will function far more efficiently if it is maintained properly. If you have a ceramic or halogen hob, follow the manufacturer's instructions for cleaning it and be aware that the surface scratches easily.

Wipe over the hob after each use to remove the residue of cooking stains and bits of food. If you have a gas hob, remove the burner attachments once a week and clean them really well in hot soapy water.

Ovens can be cleaned with any number of proprietary cleaners, but many are caustic and abrasive, so exercise extreme caution when you are using them.

Always wear protective clothes—at least an apron and rubber gloves.

Make sure the room is properly ventilated to avoid a build-up of toxic fumes when cleaning with strong solutions.

Keep small children and pets out of the way, preferably in another room.

You can make your own oven cleaner, which is cheaper and less toxic:

MIX TOGETHER: One tablespoon of baking soda and half a pint (250ml) of hot water. Wipe this over the whole oven, including glass doors and shelves, then forget about it. Old burn marks will gradually disappear. Store spare solution in a clearly marked jar.

After using the oven, place a saucerful of household ammonia in the bottom of the oven while it is still warm. Once the oven has cooled completely (or the next day) remove the ammonia and dispose of it, then wipe the inside of the oven to remove grease easily. Make a paste from baking soda and water to finish off and remove really stubborn stains.

A badly marked glass door, or a stained piece of glass ovenware can also be cleaned by wiping with a damp cloth dipped in salt, The salt is slightly abrasive and can be rinsed off after 10 minutes.

Wipe down your hob or oven doors with white wine vinegar: it cuts through grease and grime and will leave glass doors looking shiny.

If you are cooking something in the oven that might bubble over like a pizza or a fruit pie, lay a baking tray on the shelf underneath to catch any drips. It's easier to clean the baking tray than the bottom of the oven.

MICROWAVES

Clean and deodorize with white wine vinegar. Simply fill a small heat-resistant bowl or ramekin dish with white wine vinegar and heat on high for one minute. Baked-on food deposits will be loosened by the steam and you can dip a cloth in the hot vinegar to remove any residues.

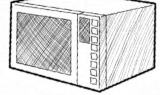

If your microwave simply needs freshening, put some lemon rind or even a couple of tablespoons of lemon juice in the microwave and heat on full for one minute.

REFRIGERATORS & FREEZERS

Every once in a while, refrigerators and freezers need a thorough clear out. It is easy to amass a collection of out of date food in the freezer, so be disciplined when shopping. Pay attention to the "use-by" date on items—even frozen food deteriorates over time.

Refrigerators should be wiped down and cleaned every week to keep them fresh.

Use a liquid mixture of baking soda and cold water as a final finish to keep it fresh. Do not use disinfectant as it may taint the flavor of the food.

Throw out anything past its sell-by date, leftover food that is more than a couple of days old, and rinse out the drawers and compartments to remove any debris.

Wipe down the door containers where you store milk and juice—it is astonishing how crusty bits of milk always accumulate there.

Once a month use a soft brush to dust the element at the back—a build-up of dust and grease hampers the efficient functioning of any refrigerator.

If you keep a drawer-by-drawer list of what is in your freezer, you will spend less time searching through it with the door open. Ice will build up less quickly, and therefore you will have to defrost it less often.

Most freezers need to be defrosted a couple of times a year, so choose a time when your freezer stocks are low. Switch the freezer off and unplug it from the mains; leave the door wide open for an hour or so before you start. Remove all the food and store it in a cool box while you tackle the ice. Place shallow bowls of recently boiled water in the freezer to help melt the ice. It is a slow process, but do not be tempted to chip at the ice with sharp or hard objects, or you may damage the interior, or worse, the freezing elements. Some people advocate the use of a hair dryer to speed things up, but exercise great caution if you do this— water and electrical appliances are a dangerous mix and a few drops of water in your hairdryer will result in a nasty electric shock.

DISHWASHER FRESHNESS

Clean out and dissolve old soap residues by adding vinegar to the soap container and letting the (empty) dishwasher run through a cycle.

If you find you have a full dishwasher and have run out of detergent powder, don't panic! Try adding baking soda to the powder holder and, if necessary, vinegar in place of rinse aid. Your crockery should emerge sparkling clean.

SINKS

Remove rust marks from stainless steel sinks by rubbing with a little lighter fluid.

Use a plastic washing-up bowl in your sink, as it provides a cushion for the crockery and saves water. Once a week fill the bowl with warm water and a couple of drops of household bleach to disinfect it. You could also drop in your washing–up brushes and cleaning cloths for a soak.

Clean your kitchen cloths and brushes by putting them in the dishwasher once a week—the heat will kill germs and leave them fresh.

BANISHING SMELLS

A smelly waste container is an unattractive feature in any kitchen. It will also harbor germs and attract flies, so empty the it before it becomes full to overflowing. And make sure that it is cleaned inside and out once a week to guard against unpleasant odors and to keep it clean. Sprinkle a little baking soda in the bottom before fitting a plastic liner, and this will help absorb nasty smells.

If the summer heat makes your waste container smell unpleasant, try sprinkling the inside with a generous amount of salt.

CANNY KITCHEN TIPS

Come home to a fresh-smelling kitchen after a few days away by leaving half a lemon in a bowl in the kitchen.

To remove the smell of fish or onion from your hands, dampen them, then rub well with salt. Wash and rinse in running water. Alternatively, try washing your hands with lemon juice, then rinsing them.

If you have broken a glass, use a piece of bread to pick up the tiny, almost invisible shards from work surfaces or hard floors. (Make sure it's a fairly thick slice!) Some people use a kitchen cleaning cloth, but with bread there is no temptation to rinse it out as there is with a cloth, thereby accidentally cutting yourself on the shards of glass.

Vacuum or thermos flasks can become stale if they are left unused, so before you go off on a picnic, make sure you leave time to freshen your thermos. Put one tablespoon of vinegar and one level teaspoon of salt into the flask and shake well. Rinse out thoroughly with clean water.

Another method of freshening up a vacuum flask is to place two tea-spoons of baking soda in an empty flask and fill the flask with recently boiled water. Leave to soak overnight, then wash in soapy water and rinse with warm water.

If your grater has lost its edge, sharpen it by rubbing the blades with sandpaper.

Clean a stained carafe or decanter by adding a few grains of rice and pouring in a little white wine vinegar. Swirl the mixture around: the rice is gently abrasive and will loosen red wine stains, especially in inaccessible nooks in crystal or cut glass items. Rinse out well with warm water and leave to air dry.

BATHROOMS

Bathrooms endure heavy traffic, frequent use, and a great deal of water-based punishment, so to keep them clean and fresh they need daily attention. Make sure you know what your bath is made of—is it acrylic, glass fiber, or vitreous enamel? Treatment will vary accordingly. Acrylic baths are easily scratched, and the color of glass fiber baths will fade if treated with abrasive cleaners.

Bathrooms are regularly steamed and soaked, so they need daily airing to prevent the formation of mildew and mold. Open the window or leave the extractor fan running after you've taken a shower or bath. Run the cold water first, then the hot to limit the formation of condensation.

Lighten your load by storing your cleaning items in or near the bathroom, rather than carrying them from the kitchen or utility room every time you need to use them. Have a separate pair of rubber gloves for bathroom use.

Before you begin to clean the bathroom, run some hot water to build up some steam. This will loosen grime, scum, and mildew, and make the whole cleaning process quicker and easier.

Remove limescale from chrome taps and plugholes by wiping down with white wine vinegar. Rinse off, and dry and polish with a paper towel. Alternatively, rub half a lemon over the taps, then rinse and polish which will give the bathroom a fresh lemony aroma rather than leaving a lingering smell of vinegar.

Rub a little petroleum jelly or baby oil on your soap dish to prevent the soap sticking to it.

If you are plagued by misty mirrors, try rubbing a little shaving foam over the mirror before you begin your ablutions, then polish it off with a dry cloth. As the steam builds up in the bathroom, your mirror will remain free from mist.

Wash your tooth mugs at least once a week. The mixture of old toothpaste and damp conditions usually means they are a breeding ground for bacteria.

The same is true of toothbrushes. Train your children to clean them properly after use, and leave them to air dry. Change toothbrushes after three months of use.

It will surely surprise nobody to learn that toilet brushes harbor germs and tiny bits of feces, however much bleach you use in cleaning the toilet. The brush is then thrust back into its container, where bacteria multiply freely. So, clean your toilet brush and its holder every time you clean the toilet.

- Always flush clean water over the brush after use.
- Once you have cleaned the toilet, add some bleach and leave the brush to stand in the bowl for an hour or so before replacing it in its container.
- Clean out the container with a solution of bleach and water, then tip this away into the toilet.

Denture cleaning tablets are an unlikely, but highly effective toilet cleaner and will help dissolve limescale. Put two into the toilet bowl and leave for an hour, before brushing and flushing. The results should be remarkable. (Note that this method will help remove limescale, but will not disinfect the toilet.)

If your bath has a really dreadful grimy ring around it, fill the bath with warm water and add two cups of biological washing powder. Leave to soak over night, then rinse and dry.

BEDROOMS

Bedrooms should be aired every day, even if it is only for ten minutes. Everybody perspires as they sleep, usually losing as much as a pint of water every night, so peel back the sheets and leave the bed to air for half an hour before you make it in the morning.

Always make the bed before you begin cleaning the bedroom, otherwise the dust produced may cover the sheets.

Dust mites love the warm atmosphere of bedrooms, where they can comfortably feed on human skin flaked off in bed. So banish them by giving the bedroom a blast of cold air every day and by vacuuming the mattress and the area under your bed regularly.

Turn the mattress every month to ensure even wear. This is especially important if the bed is occupied by partners of unequal weights.

If your mattress smells a little musty, sprinkle some baking soda over it and leave for a couple of hours before vacuuming it off.

Spare beds look much neater when they are made up. Keep the bedding smelling fresh by tucking a fabric conditioner sheet between the sheets and don't forget to air the bed for an hour or so on the day of the guests' arrival.

Children's bedrooms are often the trickiest of all, with the floor hidden under a jumble of toys, books, clothes, and bedding. There is no easy answer to solving the perennial problem of how to make kids clean their rooms, so here are a few tips:

☞ Provide plenty of storage so that all their possessions can be put away (if only for a brief period). Use stackable plastic crates of different colors to house different toys and encourage children to put toys away when they have finished playing with them.

- ☞ Offer incentives to keep the room tidy.
- ☞ Give them a deadline and stick to it. If you need to vacuum, the floor must be clear, and the ultimate threat is that anything on the floor will be thrown out.

CLEANING UPHOLSTERY

Sofas and easy chairs are built to cope with a rough life. They withstand the weight of the heaviest visitors, often suffer from the bouncing of excited children, absorb the crumbs, spills, and slurps of the family couch potato, and we STILL expect them to maintain their good looks that made us fall in love with them in the show room.

Look after your upholstered furniture by vacuuming it once a week and giving the cushions a good shake to plump them up every day. Turn the cushions every day to make sure they "wear" evenly, and to show off the chairs and sofa to their best advantage.

If you really value your soft furnishings, try to minimize the amount of food that is consumed on or around them. Fingers greasy from chips will not enhance the good looks or help prolong the life of your furniture.

Remove pet hairs quickly and easily by putting on a rubber glove and running your hand along the cushions in one direction to gather stray hairs and fibers. An alternative method is to use a barely damp chamois leather. The best way to prevent them, of course, is to keep your pets off your favorite chairs.

It is inevitable that soft furnishings will need more than just a good vacuum now and then, but before you start major cleaning work check that:

☞ You are aware of the properties of the covering material on your upholstery.

☞ You know about the nature of the stain and how best to treat it.

☞ You avoid damaging the material by testing proprietary solvents on a small inconspicuous area to check that the solvent will not bleach the material or cause dyes to run.

New stains and dirt such as mud can often be removed with shaving foam. Spray a little on the affected area, then bash the area with a dry cloth to avoid leaving watermarks, and dry with a hairdryer. If you don't have any shaving foam, try the following recipe.

UPHOLSTERY CLEANER: Mix 4 fl oz (125 ml) of mild detergent with 1 pint (500 ml) boiling water. Cool it until it gels, then whip with a hand beater or electric whisk until it produces a stiff foam. Use in the same way as shaving foam.

Oil or grease stains should be sprinkled with corn starch, talcum powder or fuller's earth, all of which will absorb the stain. Rub well and leave the powder until the stain is absorbed. Brush or vacuum off, then wipe with a damp cloth and allow to dry.

Velvet or corduroy upholstery can be cleaned by wiping with a clean, barely damp chamois leather. Use dry cleaning fluid to treat any stains.

Curtains and blinds should be vacuumed to remove dust. Roller blinds and vertical blinds can be vacuumed with the upholstery attachment. Rotate Venetian blinds so that the slats are angled one way and wipe with a damp duster or vacuum; then turn the slats the other way and do the same again.

FLOORS

Vacuum the carpets in your house at least once a week, and probably more often in areas with heavy traffic, such as the hall and landing. An annual steam clean or shampoo will make them last longer and really helps to revive a faded or "tired-looking" carpet.

Consider hiring a steam cleaner, as the carpet will dry more quickly and steaming will remove more dirt than a simple shampoo job. If your carpets really need treatment, consider hiring a professional carpet cleaner to ensure a really good job.

Carpet spills usually involve wine, coffee, or tea, and it is advisable to clean them up immediately.

Mop up spilled coffee and then sponge the area with a solution of warm water and liquid soap (or carpet shampoo). Rinse with cold water. Alternatively, sponge the area with baking soda and water.

A dried coffee stain may be removed with a solution of one-part glycerine to one-part water.

Treat red wine by mopping up the excess, then pour club soda on the stain. Use an old (white) towel to absorb the excess moisture, but be generous with the club soda, which will flush out the red stain.

Beer spillages may be treated in the same way, and may also be cleared up by sponging with warm water. Blot well to absorb the moisture and use carpet shampoo on any remaining stain.

Put an ice cube on chewing gum to harden it, then pick the gum off the carpet. Use white spirit or methylated spirit to clear off the rest. Rinse with cool water then blot dry.

An egg makes a daunting mess if dropped, but an effortless way to clear it up is to cover it with salt. This will cause it to congeal and it will be much easier to scrape up.

If you spill soot on your carpet, cover it immediately with salt and brush it up with a stiff brush. Repeat the process until the stain has disappeared. Do not be tempted to use water, as it will help soak it into the pile.

If you discover that moths have infested a carpet, spread a damp towel over the area and iron it with a hot iron. The heat and steam will destroy the worms and eggs.

If your carpet has become dented by heavy furniture, put an ice cube on each dent and leave to melt and dry. When it is dry, vacuum thoroughly and watch the pile spring back into place.

Hard floor hints

Hard floors are, to an extent, easier to look after, partly because spills are less of a problem. However, they still need regular care to keep them looking pristine and to ensure that they last well. Sensitive proprietary microfiber cloths which attract dust, remove grime very efficiently, and can be used in between major cleaning sessions.

Use a damp cloth and baking soda to remove heel marks. This is mildly abrasive, yet gentle enough not to damage the floor.

Ceramic tiles can be cleaned every week with a mild detergent solution and a mop and bucket. If possible use two buckets, one with the soapy solution, the other with warm clean water for rinsing. Polish dry with a chamois leather.

Concrete floors are easy; just sweep them regularly, or use the hard floor attachment on the vacuum cleaner to remove the worst dust and dirt.

Stone floors should also be swept regularly and can be washed every month or so with a solution of washing soda in warm water. (Use a handful of washing soda crystals in a bucket of warm water.)

Cork tiles are usually sealed with varnish or sealant, and can be cleaned with a damp mop. Waxed cork will benefit from regular sweeping and the occasional application of wax or liquid polish.

Sweep vinyl floors regularly to prevent a build-up of dirt. Mop with a warm solution of detergent to remove sticky stains and rinse with clear water. Leave to dry naturally.

Wood floors with a waxed finish should be swept regularly with a soft broom, but should not be washed with a mop as water may soak in and distort the wood. Wipe up sticky spills with a damp cloth. Wax the floor by applying wax polish paste every month or so. After a time, the polish will build up and simply look dull, at which point it must be removed by a cloth dipped in white spirit, followed by a new application of wax.

Sealed wood floors can be damp-mopped and should be polished with wax or emulsion polish to maintain the floor's shine.

FURNITURE

Wooden furniture does not need to be polished every week. Simply wipe over with a damp duster to remove the build-up of dust. As with any item, it is important to know exactly what it is made of, so check manufacturer's instructions on new items. Large wooden items will benefit from an application of wax polish every month or so.

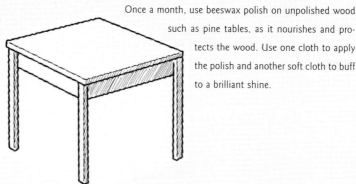

Once a month, use beeswax polish on unpolished wood such as pine tables, as it nourishes and protects the wood. Use one cloth to apply the polish and another soft cloth to buff to a brilliant shine.

If you have valuable furniture that you want to keep from fading, position it away from bright sunlight, especially if it is upholstered. Old fabrics are especially prone to losing their color under direct sunlight.

Cane or wicker furniture is often hard to dust. Use a clean, slightly damp paintbrush to dust tricky areas. Once a year, clean with warm soapy water and rinse with cold salted water. Choose a sunny day, because it is simplest to dry such large items outside.

Remove candle grease from a wooden surface by softening it with a hair dryer, then using a paper towel to absorb the stain. Wipe with a mild solution of vinegar and warm water, then dry and polish. (Please note this may not be suitable for varnished surfaces.)

Keep a brown felt-tipped pen handy to cover any scratches on wooden furniture.

METALS

Proprietary metal polishes are probably best for most metal cleaning, but approach valuable objects with care, as over-zealous cleaning could potentially ruin them.

A paste of three parts salt to one part lemon juice can be used to shine slightly tarnished brass or copper, but a proprietary cleaner will also do a good job and will leave a protective coating on the surface that reduces the build-up of tarnish.

Wipe off coal dust and soot from fire irons with a damp cloth when they are cool.

Silver cutlery can be treated with a silver dip, which will remove mild tarnishing, but do not use this on Sheffield plate, which must be treated more gently by washing in soapy water and polishing with a soft cloth.

Line a plastic bowl with aluminum foil (shiny side up) and add hot water and a handful of soda crystals. Add solid silver items (including jewelry) and leave them to soak for up to five minutes. The foil attracts the dirt, and your silver will regain its sparkle. Rinse everything and dry with a soft cloth.

TRICKS OF THE TRADE

Get a really good doormat. A huge percentage of household grime enters via shoes, so an efficient, unavoidable mat will reduce the amount of time you spend cleaning the floors and will lessen wear and tear on carpets. Consider asking everyone to remove their shoes on entering the house.

Keep your old toothbrushes so you can use them on the following:

- Clean the fiddly bits on a grater by brushing the wrong side with a toothbrush. Toothbrushes are also useful for cleaning the tricky bits on household appliances such as food processors.
- Keep one with your bathroom cleaning equipment for scrubbing mold or discoloration out of grout on your bathroom tiles.
- Keep one with your jewelry as it is perfect for cleaning rings and chains. Simply use hot soapy water and polish items dry with a soft cloth.

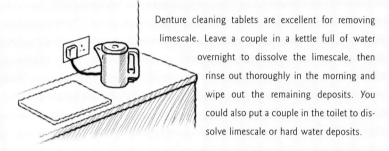

Denture cleaning tablets are excellent for removing limescale. Leave a couple in a kettle full of water overnight to dissolve the limescale, then rinse out thoroughly in the morning and wipe out the remaining deposits. You could also put a couple in the toilet to dissolve limescale or hard water deposits.

If you keep plastic wrap (clingfilm) in the fridge it will be much easier to handle.

Metal cans of shaving foam often leave rusty and unsightly marks in bathrooms. Prevent this by applying a light coat of clear nail varnish to the bottom of the can. Water will not be able to penetrate the metal, which, in turn, will not rust.

Remove limescale from taps by soaking a paper towel in vinegar and wrapping it around a tap in a plastic bag. Secure it with an elastic band and leave over night. When you remove it in the morning, the limescale will just fall off. (Please note, do not use this method on plated taps, especially gold ones as the vinegar may mark the surface.)

Dampen your duster and it will pick up dust far more efficiently.

Clean silk flowers by putting them in a large paper bag with some salt. Shake everything vigorously, then pull out dust-free flowers. Use a hair dryer (on low) to blow dust off artificial flowers.

Don't lose your rings when you are washing up or cleaning. Remove them and hang them from a large safety pin clipped to your clothing.

Woodlice love damp places, so sprinkle their hide-out with talcum powder or even baking powder to deter them. They also like houseplants, so keep houseplants off windowsills and ledges.

Small creatures which infest our living space can most easily be deterred by thorough vacuuming. Spiders, ants, and silverfish hide under furniture, so make sure that you move the furniture and vacuum underneath chairs, sofas, and beds.

Keep a piece of white chalk in drawers of silver cutlery or with silver jewelry. They will retain their shine for longer.

COOKING & EATING

Whether you love cooking or loathe it, most of us must face the daily task of foraging for something to eat, and the kitchen is probably the first port of call. Whatever your culinary inclinations, check out these hints to maximize your potential in the kitchen and save you time and money. There is no point in purchasing expensive ingredients if you then store them incorrectly and they deteriorate and lose their freshness. Spoiled food is wasted food, which equals wasted money.

STORAGE & ORGANIZATION

A kitchen that is poorly organized is really difficult to work in. If you leave the work surfaces scattered with packets and cans (not to mention the mail, sports kit, comics, and worse), it will take ages to find anything. Clear up the clutter and organize the kitchen cupboards logically.

For instance, it makes sense to store food in the cupboards nearest to the hob and oven so that you do not have to trek round the kitchen to reach them.

Get some storage jars for rice, pasta, flour, dried pulses, and anything else that tends to pour out of an opened packet. Cupboard shelves covered in tasty morsels attract vermin.

Some canned or bottled items must be refrigerated once open. Canned items must be decanted into an airtight container and should not be stored in an open can in the fridge.

Clean the cupboards and shelves of the pantry once a month with a damp cloth.

Be especially careful to keep sweet things such as sugar and biscuits, sealed up or else they are likely to attract a procession of ants.

If you are troubled by ants, draw a thick chalk line or pour a line of flour around the edges of the cupboard shelves, or better still around the points where ants are likely to enter your home, such as doors, and window frames. Ants will not cross a line of flour or chalk. Both are especially useful ant deterrents in the kitchen, as unlike proprietary ant killers, they are non-toxic.

SHOPPING TIPS

Make sure that everything you buy is as fresh as possible, so take note of "use-by" dates. When filling up your store cupboard, move those foodstuffs that are about to expire to the front of the shelves and use them first.

When you embark on a large grocery shopping trip, make a list and try to stick to it. Without one, you almost certainly buy more on impulse and spend more.

Supermarkets are the best places to take advantage of bulk-buy offers. Try shopping with a friend and splitting bulk buys in half if you feel you will not use the larger quantities offered. It is usually worth taking up offers on half-price toilet paper, kitchen roll or washing powder, for example, as eventually, it will all get used! Be more wary about fresh food, however. Will you be able to eat that large tray of melons before they deteriorate? It is also worth considering whether you have room to store large amounts of cut-price bargains.

Get to know your local shops, especially if you are catering for one or two. Although their prices may not be as competitive as a supermarket, it is often cheaper for small items such as milk and bread, especially when you consider the cost of a car journey to your nearest superstore.

Don't go shopping on an empty stomach—you are bound to buy more! Take a cool box or bag with you if you know you are going to buy frozen food, and get it home as quickly as possible. Never leave your shopping in a hot car while you go off somewhere else.

FOOD HYGIENE

The first step on the way to good food hygiene is to make sure that your working area is clean (see A Clean House for tips on how to keep the kitchen sparkling).

When handling meat be scrupulous about hygiene. Most food poisoning results from carelessness or from allowing food to stand at temperatures between 41°F (5°C) and 140°F (60°C) when bacteria will multiply.

Always wash your hands after you have handled raw meat. Dry them on a paper towel or hand towel. Do not use the tea towels as there is a danger that bacteria will transfer from the towels to utensils.

Dedicate one board to meat preparation alone and make sure you clean it thoroughly immediately after use. Wash it in hot soapy water using a scrubbing brush, then rinse in hot water and leave to air dry.

COLD STORE

Set your fridge to about 39°F (4°C) and the freezer to 0°F (–18°C). Store cooked meat at the bottom of the fridge. Not only is this the coldest part, but it will ensure that meat juices do not drip onto other items stored below and contaminate them.

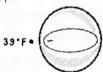

Use the cheese drawers and vegetable drawers. They help keep vegetables fresh and crisp and the cheese drawers will seal in the odor of smelly cheese (up to a point).

Do not overload your refrigerator. Air must be able to circulate between the shelves and between the items themselves, so don't cram everything in tightly.

If you know you need to store more food than normal, turn the temperature down for a couple of hours before you add the extra food.

There are few foods that actually benefit from being stored too long in plastic wrap (clingfilm) as it makes them "sweat" and deteriorate. It is sensible to repackage meat when you get it home. Use a few plastic storage boxes, perhaps with different colored lids so you can distinguish between their contents. Do not store different meats together and NEVER store cooked and raw food in the same container. Note the "use-by" date on a label on the lid.

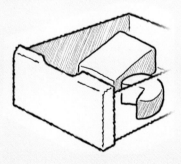

FREEZING TIPS

❄ Never refreeze meat
once it has been
thawed.

❄ When freezing meat,
make sure you expel
as much air as
possible from the
packaging. Fat is
oxidized by oxygen
left in the packaging,

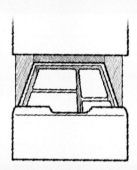

and after prolonged storage, the meat will taste off.

❄ If you are freezing several steaks or chops, interleave them
with plastic film or baking paper that will enable you to
separate them later if you want to defrost them one at
a time.

❄ Try to keep a sliced loaf of bread in the freezer as back-up
—you never know when you might need it. A frozen loaf
is especially useful if you return late at night, or from
holiday and need instant snacks—just pop a few slices in
the toaster!

* Before you freeze food, turn the controls to their lowest settings so the food will freeze as quickly as possible.

* Cool food that you are about to freeze as quickly as possible by standing it in a cold area of the kitchen or in a container of cold water. Do not put it in the refrigerator, however, as this will create condensation and raise the temperature.

* Label everything—once frozen, one delicious stew looks much like another! Either use labels or a permanent marker.

* Use ice cube trays to freeze stocks and sauces. Once frozen, transfer the cubes to bags and label them clearly.

* Homemade baby food is economical, nutritious, and easy to make. Simply puree whatever your baby needs and freeze in ice cube trays. Re-heating three or four cubes in a microwave is a quick way to feed a young baby.

* If you have a power cut, avoid opening your freezer. Food will remain frozen for at least 24 hours if left undisturbed, but it will defrost very quickly if you open the door to check on it. If the contents of your freezer defrost, you must throw out everything you cannot immediately eat.

Do not freeze

※ Milk, and milk products such as yogurt, sour cream, or mayonnaise should not be frozen. They will all separate.

※ Hard boiled eggs become leathery after freezing. (Egg whites freeze well, however, and can be frozen in an ice cube tray, which makes them easy to retrieve when you need them. Thaw them slowly in the fridge when you re-use them.)

※ Carbonated drinks may explode in extreme cold.

※ Pasta loses its texture when frozen.

Microwave tips

Microwave ovens can be used to speed up a number of kitchen tasks, but must be used properly. Always check that food is cooked through before consuming it. If you are cooking a prepared meal, follow the packaging instructions.

Never use a metal dish, or anything with a metal trim in a microwave oven. Take care not to leave a metal utensil in a bowl of food that you are about to put in the microwave. Microwaves disturb the magnetic field in metal and will cause sparks and alarming popping noises.

It is worth investing in a set of microwave containers that are specially constructed to withstand the properties of microwave heat. Plastic ice cream containers or storage boxes may be used, but if the food becomes too hot it may distort the plastic.

Cover sauces, soups, and casseroles—not only will this mean they are heated more efficiently, but it will also prevent them spitting all over the inside of the oven. A cover will help retain the moisture, too. Paper coffee filters are excellent as they absorb fat and liquid and can be thrown away when you're finished.

It is all too easy to overcook food in the microwave, so if in doubt, err on the side of undercooking, check the food, and then continue to cook in short bursts until done.

Always stir food and allow to stand for a minute or so before eating. In this way, the heat will diffuse more evenly throughout the dish.

Stale crackers, cereals, and nuts will improve if given a short burst in the microwave. Line a bowl with kitchen paper, pour in the stale breakfast cereal and heat for 30 seconds. Leave to cool before eating. Lay crackers in a single layer and heat for 20 seconds on high. Peanuts can be treated in the same way as breakfast cereals, but sprinkle a little coarse salt on the kitchen paper first.

Microwaves can be used to ripen a number of fruits and vegetables, such as avocados. Heat them on low for two minutes, turning once. Be careful not to over-do it, as the inside will turn black.

Before peeling peaches or tomatoes, prick the skin with a fork and microwave each item for about a minute (less for small fruit). Leave for five minutes and then the skin should come off easily.

Unusual uses for the microwave

Fabric shoes can be washed in the washing machine and, as long as they contain no metal parts around the eyelets, for example, dried out on a gentle microwave setting.

Wet hand towels can also benefit from instant drying in this way.

If you find you have run out of underwear or socks and find them still soggy in the washing machine, pop them in the microwave. (Please note: this is not suitable for drying underwired bras, which may have metal parts.)

Dry fresh flowers or herbs. Place a single layer of herbs between two pieces of kitchen towel and microwave on high for two minutes. Leave to stand for a minute and repeat until the herbs are dry. Flowers, being larger, will take a little longer, but the basic process is the same; a rose, for example, takes three minutes.

EMERGENCY CATERING TIPS

Everyone has been faced with an influx of extra visitors at some point, and probably tackled the attendant problem of how to feed them. Or worse, how do you cope when something you have cooked for a roomful of guests turns out burned, or is dropped on the way to the table? A well-stocked freezer or refrigerator can help out in these situations, as can the phone number of the nearest pizza delivery service! Try to keep your sense of humor and don't panic.

Even if you hate cooking and prefer take-outs or fast food, keep a basic supply of vital foodstuffs so that you can conjure up something to eat if your usual dining service deserts you. Store cupboard basics depend largely on taste, but some dried food (rice or pasta), a couple of cans of chopped tomatoes, dried herbs, garlic, canned or dried vegetables and stock cubes are enough to make a tasty pasta sauce. The less ambitious may prefer to stock just a few cans of baked beans.

Even the largest roast chicken will only feed six adults, so keep a packet of frozen chicken breasts in the freezer. If more guests arrive, defrost the breasts and roast them with the chicken. If you slit the skin on the main bird, you will be able to pad it out with a couple more breasts. Remember to adjust the overall cooking time accordingly.

Keep a supply of good vanilla ice cream and frozen berries in the freezer. You can use these to produce an instant desert. The berries will defrost very quickly in a microwave and can be puréed with a hand blender to form a delicious sauce in a matter of minutes.

Pasta and rice are probably the most versatile store cupboard ingredients and can pad out almost any meal.

Many dishes can be stretched by turning them into a stew or casserole. Add vegetables and potatoes to a stewing dish with the meat, add some stock or wine, a few herbs, and leave to cook in the oven. .

If a vegetarian turns up by surprise, use pasta, a can of tomatoes, a garlic clove, and an onion to produce a delicious pasta neapolitana.

Does your sauce remain stubbornly lumpy? Try using a whisk to smooth out the lumps. If this fails, pour the whole thing through a sieve, or put it in the blender.

Lost the corkscrew? Turn the bottle of wine upside down and bang sharply with a shoe or book. The cork will gradually move out of the neck of the bottle and when there is enough to grasp, you can pull it out.

MASKING COOKING SMELLS

To hide the smell of frying onions, put a sheet of wet newspaper close to the burners of your hob and it will absorb the odor.

Fresh orange or lemon peel cooked in the oven at gas mark 4/350°F/180°C for 10 to 15 minutes will fill the kitchen with a delightful orange fragrance.

If your chopping board begins to smell of fish, onion or garlic, rub it all over with half a cut lemon, which will neutralize the aroma.

Add a little parsley to the saucepan when cooking sprouts or cabbage to minimize the odor. A few bay leaves should also do the same trick and will not harm the vegetable's flavor.

Fruit & vegetable tips

Health professionals advise everyone to eat more fresh fruit and vegetables, recommending five 4 oz (100 g) portions per person per day. This really isn't so hard and will help protect you from illnesses ranging from the common cold to cancer. Here are a few hints on how to choose the best produce.

How to spot fresh produce

Citrus fruits should feel heavy for their size as this is a sign that they are full of juice. Any that seem light are probably old and dehydrated.

Shake a bunch of grapes before purchasing them. If any fall off, they aren't fresh.

Hold a melon firmly in both hands and lightly press the area around the tip—the opposite end to the stem. If it gives slightly, the melon is ripe.

Don't store melons in the refrigerator unless they are kept in a sealed container, as their aroma may taint other articles.

A pineapple is ready to eat if you can easily pull out a leaf from the top of the fruit bulb.

If blackberries and raspberries still have the hull attached, they were under-ripe when picked and may lack flavor.

Apples and pears should have a firm skin, without any hint of wrinkling or shrinkage.

Bananas should be yellow with few black marks. If they're green, they're not ready to eat; the more black marks, the riper and softer they are.

When you get fresh fruit and vegetables home, remove them from any plastic wrapping. They will stay fresh longer and taste better if air can circulate around them.

FRUIT

Chefs have been utilizing fruit to enhance the flavors of other foods for centuries. Check out these useful tips.

An average lemon yields three tablespoons of juice (3 fl oz or 75 ml).

An average orange contains about six tablespoons (5 fl oz or 150 ml) of juice.

If you only need a small amount of lemon or orange juice, pierce the fruit with a cocktail stick or skewer and squeeze out what you need. The rind will seal up again and the fruit will remain fresh.

Lemon juice is a subtle yet vital ingredient and will enhance many dishes.

- ✳ It helps to keep fish white during cooking. If you are cooking an oily fish such as mackerel, squeeze a little lemon juice over it while broiling or grilling.
- ✳ Add a squeeze of lemon to mushrooms when they are being fried—it will bring out the flavor.
- ✳ When cooking whole onions, cabbage, or cauliflower, add lemon to the water to remove the all-pervading smell.

❋ Add a squeeze of lemon to a small
tub of single cream to make sour cream.

Make instant apple sauce by coring an apple and placing
the whole fruit, skin on, in the microwave. Heat on high for a minute,
or until the flesh is soft enough to scoop out. Scoop into a bowl and
add sugar to taste if you like.

All fruits and vegetables excrete a plant hormone called ethylene as they
mature, and apples, bananas, and tomatoes continue to excrete this
even after they are harvested. If you want to ripen unripe fruit such as
avocados or melons, place in a paper bag with an apple or ripe tomato,
and keep it at room temperature. The unripe fruit will ripen quickly, but
don't forget it, or you will find a moldy, mushy bag!

To skin tomatoes or grapes, plunge them into a bowl of recently boiled
water for a minute or two. Make a slit in the skin when you remove the
fruit and it will peel off easily.

VEGETABLES

Onions are one of the most useful and widely used vegetables, but preparation can be a tearful and sometimes slightly noxious experience. Try storing onions in the refrigerator an hour or so before you need them. Their aroma will be released far more slowly when they are chilled and will be less likely to make your eyes water. Other methods include peeling them under running water, or sucking a spoon while you do it.

If you find that your hands smell of onions after you have prepared them, try any one of these methods to remove the smell.

※ Rub your hands with coffee grounds, then rinse off with cold water.

※ Dampen your hands and rub them with salt. Rinse off.

※ If your kitchen knives harbor the smell of onion or fish, one folk remedy advocates plunging them into the earth several times before washing as usual.

※ Try holding onto a stainless steel item such as a sieve while rinsing your hands under cold running water.

Add a little milk to the pan in which you are boiling cauliflower or potatoes; it will keep both vegetables really white.

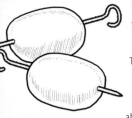

Cut down the cooking time of baked potatoes by spearing them with a skewer to help conduct the heat evenly through them.

To make really crispy roast potatoes, boil for ten minutes in salted water, drain, then sprinkle liberally with flour. Add to a prepared roasting tray with really hot fat and roast as usual for about an hour.

Dried herbs are a really useful addition to any store cupboard, but growing a few herbs in pots in your kitchen or in tubs in your yard is simplicity itself. Rosemary, parsley, mint, thyme, and sage will grow almost anywhere; basil and coriander may require a little more tender loving care. They can also be frozen or dried for use during the winter. Growing herbs on the kitchen windowsill will help ward off bugs and flies: mint deters ants, and sage and thyme keep moths away.

Parsley can be chopped finely and very quickly using kitchen scissors.

Add a sprig of mint to old potatoes when they are being boiled. This will improve the flavor.

Revive a limp lettuce by sitting it in some icy water for 20 minutes before using it in a salad.

Mushrooms stay fresh when wrapped in paper, such as kitchen paper or a brown paper bag, rather than plastic packaging. They do not need to be kept in the coldest part of the refrigerator.

Mushrooms often shrink when they're fried. Pour boiling water over them before you cook them and they will retain their size.

MEAT & FISH

Although most meat is purchased in pre-packaged trays from the super-market these days, it is worth knowing how to recognize really fresh, top quality items. Always buy the freshest meat and fish possible.

Beef should be firm to the touch, red, and slightly bloody; if it is begin-ning to go brown, it is getting old and probably drying out.

Lamb should be pinkish—the lighter the color, the younger the animal. If the fat on frozen lamb is brittle white, it has probably been in the freezer too long.

Pork should also be firm and smooth to the touch, with a pink hue. It should be slightly moist, but certainly not wet.

Use a craft knife to score the fat on pork, then season liberally with salt to make really good crackling. Make the slashes quite close together then rub the salt in. If you are really organized, do this the night before, wipe off in the morning, then rub the skin with cooking oil to achieve perfect results.

Chickens should be plump with a white skin (unless you are buying a "corn-fed" bird, which will be yellow).

Any meat that smells slightly rancid or looks slimy is probably "off."

FISH

When cooking fish, wrap it in plastic wrap (clingfilm), and poach in boiling water to retain the full flavor.

Thaw frozen fish in milk, which will remove the stale frozen taste and restore a "freshly caught" flavor.

Bake fillets of fish on lettuce leaves to prevent them sticking to the baking tray and to retain moisture.

EGGS

Within a fragile egg shell lurks one of the most versatile culinary ingredients. Use these tips to ensure that you get the best use from the freshest eggs.

When buying eggs, always open the carton to check that all the eggs are intact without cracks.

When choosing eggs remember that:

❋ Fresh eggs should be heavy for their size.

❋ They should have a slightly rough shell.

❋ When broken on a plate, the yolk should be high and rounded and the white should be jelly-like.

❋ To test for freshness, put an egg in a bowl of water. A fresh egg will sink; older eggs have more air in them and are more likely to float.

If an egg is stuck to the box, simply wet the box and the egg will slip out easily.

Store eggs in the refrigerator where they will stay fresh for longer. If you keep them in the door, they will remain fresh for up to 10 days, but stored in a box in the bottom of the fridge, they will be fine for up to three weeks.

Store eggs pointed end down.

Eggs have a better flavor when used at room temperature, so take them out of the refrigerator about an hour before you need them.

Egg whites can be stored for up to a week in a refrigerator if covered in plastic wrap (clingfilm).

Unused egg yolks should be covered with a little cold water and stored in the refrigerator, where they will remain usable for several days.

Add a pinch of salt to egg whites to make them thicken faster.

To make a really light and fluffy omelet, add a pinch of cornstarch to the eggs before beating.

To prevent a boiled egg cracking, pierce the egg shell with a pin before boiling the egg. An egg is less likely to crack if it is added to cold or lukewarm water and heated up gradually. Eggs added to boiling water are more prone to cracking.

Add vinegar to the boiling water if an egg cracks, and this will stop the white spilling out.

Plunge hard-boiled eggs into cold water immediately after cooking to stop the edge of the
yolks turning black.

EDIBLE SHORTCUTS

Even the keenest cook has days when time is against them. Use these tips to make catering easier and to allow yourself time to sit down and relax with a glass of wine!

Buy packs of salad rather than whole lettuces. It saves time in washing and chopping. The same is true for pre-prepared packs of vegetables, which are topped and tailed and ready for cooking.

One of the easiest items to cook is a roast chicken: simply rub with a little butter and salt, add stuffing or a lemon, and pop it in the oven for 20 minutes per pound. Set the timer and leave it to roast.

Thin cuts of meat or fish cook more quickly than large steaks or chops.

Make good use of the deli counter to gather an interesting and tasty array of items for a quick, effortless meal.

When making scrambled eggs (one of the quickest meals ever) put the eggs in a buttered heatproof bowl over a saucepan of boiling water. They will scramble just as well and taste creamier. Best of all, there will be no stuck-on egg to remove from the saucepan!

Dairy products

If milk boils over, mask the odor by tipping some salt over the stain and then wiping it off.

When making a white sauce, add warm milk instead of cold to keep the mixture smooth.

If a recipe calls for sour cream and you don't have any, add a little lemon juice to single or double cream.

If your cream refuses to whip up properly, try adding a drop of lemon juice to it. Cream will whip better if the bowl and utensils are cold. For really light whipped cream, add a couple of drops of iced water just before the final stage of whipping.

When making a dessert topping, whip cream with honey instead of sugar and it will stay stiffer for longer.

Cheese must be stored in a cool place and while the top of a refrigerator is fine, a cool, dark place in a pantry will preserve the flavor better. Wrap your cheese in a clean muslin cloth dampened with white wine vinegar. This will keep it fresh and prevent crustiness and mold forming.

PIZZA AND PASTA

Pizza and pasta dishes are very popular and if you follow these tips they can be even simpler and easier to make.

Butter the rim of a pan in which you cook rice or pasta to prevent it from boiling over.

Use lots of water to cook lasagne noodles so the pasta has plenty of room to expand. To prevent tearing, cook at a moderate yet constant boil. Once pasta has been added to boiling water, start timing when the water returns to a boil. Use a wood or plastic spoon, or heat-resistant rubber spatula to stir occasionally while cooking. Stir gently. Boil the pasta for less time if you intend to use it in a baked dish. Slowly drain the water and slide the lasagne gently into a colander. Drain well. Place in a covered container right away to prevent it from sticking together.

Kitchen scissors cut through pizza more quickly and cleanly than a knife. And, they don't scratch your pizza pan.

Make pizza dough in double batches and freeze half. You can even roll out the extra dough, fit it into a pizza pan, and freeze it flat for a head start on a fast meal.

The intensity of tomato sauce may be adjusted by adding a small amount of garlic and crushed peppercorn. Its "bite" is increased by adding balsamic vinegar.

Create an oil sauce for pasta instead of tomato by using extra virgin olive oil, herbs/spices, and fresh garlic.

DESSERTS

For a moister banana nut bread, pour half of the batter in the baking pan, spread pineapple tidbits (drained) over the batter, then cover with the remaining batter.

To cool a loaf of bread, remove the loaf from the pan immediately and place on a wire rack.

To cut a cake neatly through decorative icing, cut it with dental floss.

When a cake recipe calls for flouring the baking pan, use a bit of the dry cake mix instead, and there won't be any white mess on the outside of the cake.

To dress up cakes and pies, place a doily on top, then sprinkle over powdered sugar and remove.

When making cookies, always use unsalted butter, which gives the cookies a lighter texture.

To prevent cookies from spreading when baking, refrigerate the dough and the baking sheet for a couple of minutes before baking.

Add a pinch of baking soda to your frosting to keep it moist and prevent cracking.

Stuff a miniature marshmallow in the bottom of a sugar cone to prevent ice cream drips.

For a practically fat-free crust, substitute frozen filo pastry for traditional pie crust. Thaw as directed, lift two leaves from the stack and center in the pie pan sprayed with nonstick cooking spray. Lay two more leaves in the pan at right angles to the first, then two more to fill gaps, until the pan is fully lined. Fill and bake the pie as directed.

To melt chocolate, place broken pieces in a bowl with a knob of butter. Microwave on high for 30 seconds. Stir. Return to the microwave and heat and stir in 30 second intervals until the chocolate reaches a smooth consistency.

Add a pinch of sugar when making waffles and pancakes to help them brown more quickly when cooking.

Use a turkey baster to squeeze pancake batter onto the hot griddle to get perfectly shaped pancakes every time.

The best way to line a cake pan with parchment paper is to place the pan on a sheet and use a pencil to trace around the bottom. Cut it out and fit into the greased pan. Cut a strip to line the edge of the cake pan and grease the paper before filling with batter and baking. Cool the cake on a wire rack for 15 minutes after baking. Invert the cake and remove the parchment paper.

When baking cookies, line a cookie sheet with parchment paper, and place the rounds of dough on it. When the first batch of cookies is done, slide the parchment with the baked cookies off the cookie sheet. Repeat with a second batch.

Always chill pastry dough before rolling and cutting, and always chill it again afterwards, before baking, to further relax the gluten.

For a flakier pastry crust, substitute one teaspoon vinegar for one teaspoon of the cold water.

When cutting a cake filled with cream, first dip the knife in hot water so that none of the filling sticks to it.

Brush some beaten egg over pie crust before baking to give a brown, glossy finish.

Coat hands with oil or water before pressing down sticky desserts to prevent sticking.

To stabilize whipped cream, add two tablespoons of nonfat dry milk to every cup of whipping cream before you whip it.

Soupy, whipped cream can be saved by adding an egg white, then chilling thoroughly and beating again.

Yeast lasts longer if kept in the refrigerator and even longer in the freezer. Place in a plastic container and mark the date of purchase.

LEFTOVERS

Take advantage of any leftovers that are still useable.

If you baked too much cake, for instance, offer to send some home with your guests. Remember, cake will also freeze well.

Slice leftover rolls and breads, spread with softened butter, and freeze them wrapped in foil. Reheat them easily in the oven. Remove the foil and they will be ready to eat.

To use up leftover egg yolks, poach them until firm, then cool them and put them through a sieve. They are good for salads and soup garnishes.

Use the liquid from canned vegetables in soups, sauces, stews and casseroles, and for making white sauce for creamed vegetables.

Use celery tops to flavor meats, stews, soups, and stuffings.

Leftover veggies? Use them in salads, or in a delicious soup or omelet. If you're making fudge and the batch doesn't harden, crumble it up, refrigerate the pieces, and use them in cookies or cakes.

Don't throw away end pieces of cheese. Grate them and freeze them in a labeled, airtight bag. You can use them in recipes calling for melted cheese, such as quiche.

Add leftover sausage meat to plain pancake batter, or combine it with leftover mashed potatoes; form the mixture into patties and brown it in a frying pan.

To extend a little meat into a meal, combine any leftover meat with rice, macaroni, or spaghetti noodles.

Freeze leftover breads and rolls to use for homemade croutons or stuffing at a later date.

If your coffee has gone cold, try re-heating it in the microwave.

Save meat drippings and store them in the refrigerator. Use them for frying, sautéing, and making gravy.

WASHING-UP

After you have prepared a feast for your friends and family, make sure you clear up properly (or better still, get them to do it). Follow the old maxim of clearing as you go to make the whole job less irksome.

Do the washing-up in the right order to minimize breakages. Wash glassware first while the water is really clean and do not add other utensils or crockery until this is done. Follow this with the cutlery, then the chinaware and finally the pots and pans, leaving the most heavily soiled items until last.

Pots and pans will be easier to clean if left to soak first.

Use really hot water and plenty of liquid soap. Change the water when it becomes cool or really murky. Washing-up water should be really hot in order to kill bacteria and cut through grease. However, be careful when washing glasses or lead crystal that may crack in very hot water.

Use a washing-up bowl in the sink as this will cushion the china and glass and lessen damage.

TRICKS OF THE TRADE

Keep butter and margarine wrappers folded in the refrigerator for greasing baking tins and trays.

Keep a sugar cube in the cheese box to preserve the freshness of your fromage.

Slice mushrooms finely by using an egg slicer.

Double cream stays fresh for longer if the cartons are stored upside down in the refrigerator.

Slice a lemon, then wrap the whole thing in plastic wrap (clingfilm) and freeze. This will provide a supply for cocktails and cold drinks and means that if you use them only rarely, you won't waste a whole lemon for the sake of one or two slices.

When baking, keep a couple of plastic bags handy. If you need to answer the phone, first stick your floury hand in a plastic bag and the phone will remain pristine and flour-free.

Leftover wine can be frozen in ice cube trays for use in stocks and sauces.

LAUNDRY

Laundry tasks are considerably less troublesome now than even 50 years ago. Ninety-eight percent of households have washing machines, and the dictates of fashion ensure that the clothes we wear are designed to be laundered frequently and easily. Household washing was once an all-day task of washing, scrubbing, rinsing, mangling, and drying, followed by an equally long job of airing and ironing. It is all a bit easier now, but looking after your clothes properly will prolong their life and keep them looking good for longer, so wash them according to the manufacturer's instructions and store them away from natural light in a cupboard free from damp and mold.

LAUNDRY HINTS

It is vital that you consider the washing instructions before you wash, dry, and iron your clothes. Read the care labels and pay attention to water temperature, detergent type, and whether an item should be given special treatment such as hand washing or dry cleaning.

If you have the space, organize you laundry by providing your family with one basket for whites and another for colored items.

Wash whites and pastels separately from strong, bright colors. Don't mix synthetics and cotton items as they require different temperatures.

Empty the pockets. Coins can foul the machine's mechanism, and old tissues will shred over all the clothes in the machine.

Wash a mixture of large and small items in one load and do not overfill the washing machine. Sheets, for example, just twist around each other if there are more than two in a load. Washing machines work by agitating clothing to remove dirt, so everything needs room to move freely.

Soaking an item will help to remove stubborn stains, but make sure that any detergent is fully dissolved before adding the clothing.

Use the right detergent for the wash and make sure you use the correct amount according to the water type, load level, and extent of staining.

Wash delicate items such as beaded tops and lacy items inside a mesh bag or pillow case. This will protect them from snagging on other garments. If you want to make a permanent delicates bag for the washing machine, use an old net curtain.

Machine-washable woolen items often emerge from the tumble drier looking irretrievably crushed. Put them in a pillow case before they go into the drier and they will keep their shape.

Turn corduroy and textured fabrics inside out to prevent them collecting fluff from other items.

Some black items fade over time, often as a result of an accumulation of soap. Soak the garment in warm water with a tablespoon of vinegar to recapture its dark good looks. (Do not soak if the item is dry-clean only.)

Hard water also dulls colored clothes. If you add a teaspoonful of salt to the detergent and then run the wash as normal, your clothes should emerge looking brighter.

Fabric conditioner reduces wrinkling on many garments, and may help to reduce the ironing pile. Remove clothes from the tumble drier immediately the cycle is finished and fold or hang them carefully. You may get away without ironing them, especially mixed fiber garments.

HAND WASHING

Items which cannot withstand very hot water or the agitation of a washing machine should be hand washed. If you suspect that the colors of a garment may run, consider hand washing it a few times before putting it in the washing machine. Use special hand-wash soap flakes and remember to rinse everything thoroughly several times. Use the washing machine's spin cycle to dry, or if you prefer, wring out the garment or wrap it in a towel to remove excess water.

The care label on many silk items advises dry cleaning only, but you can hand wash silk if you treat it gently. (If you really treasure an item, however, always abide by the instructions on the care label.) Use warm water and a detergent specifically for wool

or delicates. Once washed and rinsed, dry naturally until it is damp and then roll it tightly into a ball, seal in a plastic bag, and place in the freezer. When it is frozen, remove from the freezer and iron.

If you find there are too many suds when you begin some hand washing, sprinkle some talcum powder over the top and they will subside.

WHITES

However carefully we treat white garments, they often become slightly gray with age, but it is possible to restore brightness to your whites with judicious use of bleaching agents. Check the care labels carefully before embarking on a bleaching session.

Socks, bras, and panties can be revived by heating them in a pan of water with a few slices of lemon. Heat the water until it boils and stir with a wooden spoon to ensure even distribution of the lemons. Let it boil for 10 minutes or so and then remove everything and allow to dry.

Dilute household bleach will restore a gleaming whiteness to dull cotton or poly-cotton shirts. Dilute in accordance with the manufacturer's instructions (if in doubt use one part bleach to ten parts cold water). Mix the bleach thoroughly in a bowl of water and add the shirts a couple at a time. Leave to soak for about ten minutes (possibly longer), stirring occasionally. Keep a close eye on the mixture, because if left for too long, the bleach may turn everything yellow. Never use chlorine bleach in its neat form as it will burn holes in the fabric. Always rinse the garment thoroughly and wear rubber gloves to protect your hands.

If you have sensitive skin or allergies, cream of tartar is an effective whitener that is kinder to the skin. Add two tablespoons to a bucket of hot water. Stir well and add the clothes, leaving them to soak overnight.

Wool or silk can be treated with dilute hydrogen peroxide. Mix one part hydrogen peroxide with four parts cold water and soak the item for up to 12 hours. Rinse thoroughly.

Many items of sports equipment can be brightened by soaking in a solution of enzyme (biological) detergent and then washing as normal. Minimize dry cleaning by following these hints:

> ☞ Use a clothes brush or fluff remover to spruce up garments before you put them away.

☞ Carry a tube of proprietary all-purpose grease solvent to treat accidents quickly.

☞ When you have finished wearing a garment, check to see whether it needs attention. Sponge collars and cuffs. Leave mud to dry and then brush off.

☞ If a garment looks a little "tired," iron it before you wear it.

DRYING

Pleated skirts will retain their pleats if they are hung out to dry by the waistband, with clothes pegs clipped to the bottom of the pleats.

Save space on a washing line by acquiring a cheap plastic peg wheel for underwear. Alternatively, peg socks and underclothes to a coat hanger.

When drying duvet covers and pillow cases outside, hang them up so they form a "bag:" attach only one side to the line to allow air to enter and circulate inside it.

Hang trousers by pegging them up by the ankle end and using the weight of the waistband to minimize creases.

IRONING

Iron items that need a cool iron first and work up to those that need a hotter setting.

Preserve the colors of your clothes for longer by ironing the wrong side of garments.

If the ironing is completely dry, put a few items in the tumble drier with a wet towel for a minute. This will make everything damp enough to iron easily. Alternatively, wrap items in the wet towel to make them slightly damp, and then iron as usual.

If you need distilled water for your iron, defrost some of the ice that has formed on the walls of the freezer.

Keep the creases in trousers razor-sharp by rubbing them on the inside with a piece of wet soap, then iron on the right side.

Iron linen when it is still quite damp—a hot iron will smooth creases really easily while drying the fabric.

WARDROBES & STORING CLOTHES

It is pointless to spend good money on lovely clothes only to mistreat them by cramming them into over-stuffed drawers and undersized wardrobes. Instead of dropping your clothes in a pile on a chair (or the floor!) hang everything up at the end of the day. Pair socks and fold underwear when replacing them in the drawers, then it will be easier to find what you want when you are getting dressed.

Go through your wardrobe one or twice a year to weed out those items you no longer wear or others that are worn out. Take them to a charity store or clothes recycling bank.

Consider purchasing some drawer organizers to keep socks and underwear tidy.

If shirts and jackets keep sliding off their hangers, slip an elastic band around each end of the hanger to anchor the clothes on it.

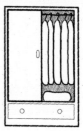

Fabric conditioner sheets will banish smells. Put one at the bottom of your laundry basket to keep odors at bay. They can also be hung in wardrobes to keep clothes smelling fresh.

Empty perfume bottles are also excellent odor-maskers. Again, put one at the bottom of the laundry basket, in your drawers, or in your wardrobe.

Keep moths away by using bay leaves, allspice berries, or cedar chips in your wardrobe. Tie up a few dried bay leaves, berries, or cedar chips in some small cotton or muslin bags and hang them among your clothes.

Don't bother ironing clothes that are going to be stored for a long period of time as they will only need ironing again before you wear them.

Avoid using fabric conditioner on clothes that are going into storage as it may accelerate mold growth.

If you must hang trousers on wire coat hangers, pad the hangar with a few sheets of newspaper to avoid creasing the trousers. They will hang better, however, if pegged to the hanger by the ends of the legs.

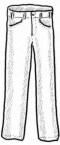

Wire coat hangers are really only suitable for light items as they can easily become distorted. Invest in some wooden hangers for suits and jackets, or consider binding two wire hangers together to strengthen them.

Linen looks fantastic when it is crisp and fresh, but creases appear all too easily. Instead of hanging linen items, store them rolled up to minimize creasing.

Angora sweaters and other fluffy woolen items often shed on to other items of clothing. Spray them occasionally with a fine mist of hairspray to prevent this.

SHOES

Do not wear the same pair of shoes two days running. Shoes need time to recover from a day's wear by drying out.
If your shoes become muddy, leave the mud to dry, then brush it off.

If your shoes are drenched in the rain, stuff them full of paper when you get home and leave somewhere warm. The paper will absorb the worst of the damp. Fabric shoes can be dried in the microwave (as long as they do not have any metal parts).

Sprinkle a little baking soda in your shoes after you have worn them to minimize odors but remember to tip it out in the morning.

Prevent sandal straps from chafing by rubbing a bar of soap over them before you put them on.

Clean canvas shoes and trainers with a toothbrush and carpet shampoo. Once the worst mud and grime has been removed, most trainers can be washed in the washing machine.

Bedding & towels

Sheets and duvet covers should be treated in the same way as clothes—always wash according to the care label. Do not try to cram too many sheets into the washing machine or dryer at once as they simply won't be cleaned properly.

Duvets and pillows should be aired regularly, either outside on a washing line, or by draping them over the bed and a couple of chairs.

Duvets, blankets, and eiderdowns should be cleaned every year. Machine-washable items will probably need to be taken to a laundromat where the industrial machines can cope with bigger loads than domestic washing machines. Do not try to wash a duvet or quilt at home, as they are so heavy when wet that the washing machine will struggle to cope, or may even break down. Alternatively, take them to the dry cleaner. Summer is probably the best time to do this as you are less likely to miss your thick bed coverings in warm weather.

Make sure you rotate your linen and use it all equally. When you return clean sheets to the cupboard, put them on the bottom of the pile. White sheets stored in an airing cupboard may develop yellow marks, so they are best kept elsewhere.

When storing matching bed sets, fold them all up and store the pillow-cases and sheets inside the duvet cover. This will save you rooting through the whole cupboard in search of the various parts of the set. Towels should be washed at 140°F (60°C) to kill germs and bacteria.

Don't wash new towels with other garments because they shed fluff and the rest of the washing becomes covered in it.

Fabric conditioner gradually erodes the absorbency of towels, so use it sparingly.

After a while, colored towels may develop a whitish bloom, which is a sign that detergent has built-up on the pile. Remove it by washing the towels as normal using equal amounts of water softener and detergent.

Prevent tea towels from shedding fluff when drying china and glass by rinsing them in a weak starch solution after washing. Ironing them not only makes them look neat, but also sterilizes them.

PILLOWS

You can tell if a pillow has reached the end of its natural life by placing it horizontally over your forearm. If it droops badly at either end it should be replaced.

Pillows will last longer if you use two pillow cases to protect them from the absorption of sweat, face cream, or perfumes.

Don't throw out old sheets that have ripped or worn. Cut them up and make coverings to use under pillow cases.

CURTAINS

Curtains are often rather heavy, especially if they are lined, so they are best cleaned by professionals. You can reduce the need for this by vacuuming the dust off them every week and perhaps hanging them outside to air once a year. If they are floor length, check the hems for extra dirt and wear and tear. Generally, heavy brocade fabrics, velvet, and lined curtains should be dry-cleaned. Take along cords, ties, and removable pelmets, too, to ensure that all the fabric is treated in the same way, if fading should occur, it will at least be even.

If the pelmet is fixed to the wall, vacuum thoroughly and treat with a little upholstery cleaner when necessary.

Be very wary about cleaning your curtains at home: curtains made up of more than one fabric (those with an outer layer and a lining, for example) may shrink at different rates, and sometimes even individual threads shrink, causing rucked seams. If in doubt, take them to a dry cleaner.

If your curtains are machine-washable:

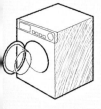

- ☞ First measure them before the wash, so they can be stretched to the correct size afterward.
- ☞ Make sure you remove all the hooks and weights. Loosen the heading tape to flatten the curtain.
- ☞ Having shaken the worst of the dust off, soak them in a bathful of cold water to remove loose dirt and grime, then wash according to the care label.
- ☞ Iron while still damp along the length of the fabric. Pay attention to the seams and press out any puckering.
- ☞ Once they are dry, replace the hooks and weights and pull the tape to the correct width before re-hanging.

Net curtains usually require more frequent attention, as dirt becomes rather obvious on them. Wash them before they look grimy to avoid permanent discoloration. As they are so light, nets can be re-hung without ironing while they are still slightly damp.

While the curtains are down, take the opportunity to clean the curtain rails really thoroughly and to clean windows and woodwork.

STAINS

When treating any stain follow a few golden rules:

- ☞ Act quickly, but be patient.
- ☞ Try the most gentle solution first; many stains react well to a bit of soap and water.
- ☞ Many stains will "set" with the application of hot or cold water, so when applying stain-removers, use lukewarm water unless the instructions advise otherwise.
- ☞ Test solvents and specialist stain removing fluids on an unobtrusive part of the garment to check that it will not burn or bleach the fabric.

☞ Do not dry your clothes in the tumble dryer until you are
sure that the stain has disappeared.

Whenever you begin to remove a stain, place a clean white towel or pad
underneath to absorb the stain and the attendant moisture. Keep renew-
ing the pad, or move it around as the stain transfers itself on to it.

If the material is stained all the way through, work from the back, or
wrong side, dabbing the stain remover on to the material with your fin-
gertips, a cotton wool pad or rag. Keep tapping at the material gently
over and over again until the stain shifts. Professional cleaners call this
method tamping, and it can be a laborious process, which explains why
really good dry cleaning is so expensive.

Keep a collection of stain removing products to help you deal with
spills. There are many proprietary cleaners available for specific stains,
but if you don't have the right one to hand, use the list below to make
a substitute. Apart from soap and detergent, and clean sponges and
absorbent cloths, a good stain-removing arsenal should include:

☞ Baking soda.
☞ Borax, a mineral that is a natural water softener and
deodorizer with mild astringent properties.

☞ Carpet shampoo.

☞ Dry cleaning fluid can be purchased in small applicator bottles and will remove grease stains very efficiently. Do not use on acetate material and follow the manufacturer's instructions.

☞ Eucalyptus oil is especially good for removing tar stains.

☞ Glycerine is available from pharmacies and works to lubricate and loosen stains. Dilute with water: one part glycerine to two parts water, apply to the stain and leave for an hour before laundering.

☞ Household ammonia must always be diluted, usually in proportion of one part ammonia to three parts water, but check the manufacturer's instructions. Sometimes you may only need to add a drop or two to a final rinse. Ammonia is toxic and gives off strong fumes, so use with caution and always protect your skin by wearing gloves.

☞ Hydrogen peroxide is also obtainable from pharmacies and available in a variety of strengths. Follow the instructions carefully to ensure the correct dilution and protect your skin from splashes by wearing rubber gloves.

☞ Methylated spirits.

☞ Washing soda crystals.

☞ White wine vinegar.

BEER OR LAGER Soak the affected garment in white vinegar. Rinse well in hot water with enzyme (biological) detergent.

BLOOD Soak fresh bloodstains in cold salted water which helps to dissolve the albumen present in blood. Alternatively, add a dessert spoonful of ammonia to one pint of water and soak a dried bloodstain in this for several hours. Afterward, wash with enzyme (biological) washing powder.

If the stain is really tough, use dilute household bleach if the fabric is suitable.

CANDLE WAX If wax has dripped on to clothing, put the garment in the freezer for an hour or so to harden the wax, which will then break off easily. Another method is to sandwich the material between two pieces of kitchen paper and apply a warm iron, which will melt the wax on to the absorbent paper. When the wax is gone, apply a small amount of methylated spirits (diluted with equal parts water for rayon and nylon) to remove any dyes that remain.

CHEWING GUM There are two schools of thought relating to chewing gum problems, so choose whichever seems most appropriate to the area of the stain and the fabric. The first is to hold the back of the fabric over the steam from a kettle until the chewing gum is soft enough to be pulled off. Steaming the fabric in this way will also help to remove the grease mark the gum leaves behind. This method is best for delicate fabrics such as velvet or corduroy. The other method is to chill the gum until it hardens. If the gum has stuck to furniture or the carpet, put an ice cube on it to harden it, then break the gum off once it has hardened. Or place the item (if the garment is tough enough) in the freezer until the gum hardens, and then remove it. The pile of velvet or corduroy is likely to break off with the frozen gum, so do not use the freezer method with these fabrics.

Egg whites are also effective on washable fabrics if you apply when the gum is still soft. Brush the egg white on, leave for 15 minutes, then pick off as much as possible before laundering. If you should be unlucky enough to get gum stuck in your hair, work a little petroleum jelly along the hairs which should loosen the gum and enable you slide it off.

CHOCOLATE If the fabric is washable, wash the item in warm soapy water. Rub glycerine into the stain and leave for an hour, then wash again in warm soapy water and rinse.

COFFEE OR TEA Coffee, tea, or cocoa can be removed by stretching the stained fabric over a small basin, dampening it with borax then pouring boiling water over the top (as long as the fabric can take this kind of treatment). Leave the garment to soak in the borax solution, then rinse and wash as normal.

COLA Rinse the stain in cold water, then work in liquid detergent from the back of the fabric and rinse. If the stain is very stubborn, sponge it with a little methylated spirits along with white vinegar and water.

FECES Pets and babies are usually the culprits! Get rid of the worst by scraping it into the toilet, holding the garment under cold running water then soaking the article in a borax solution for half an hour. Wash with enzyme (biological) detergent.

If the deposit is on a carpet, scrape off the worst and spray the stain with club soda. Make up a lather from carpet shampoo and scrub in well then rinse off with clean water. It might be sensible to add a small amount of disinfectant to this rinse.

FRUIT & VEGETABLE STAINS Berries, dark fruits, and highly colored vegetables such as beetroot contain powerful dyes.

Traditional remedies advise soaking a piece of bread in water and dabbing it on both sides of the cloth to absorb the red color. Alternatively, try dabbing with white wine vinegar, or hot milk, or use a solution of one and a half teaspoons of borax in half a pint (250ml) of water. If the stain has become fixed, put the garment over a bowl or sink and pour boiling water on it.

GREASE A stain from greasy food may be treated by an application of talcum powder, especially if the fabric is delicate or non-washable. Sprinkle it on the affected area, leave to dry for five minutes, then brush off and apply dry cleaning fluid to remove the last vestiges of the mark. Another method is to cover the stain with brown paper or kitchen paper and press with a hot iron. The paper will soak up the grease which has been melted by the iron's heat.

GRASS Soak grass-stained clothes in vinegar before laundering as usual. It will also help remove tea and coffee stains, as well as those from summer berries.

On manmade fibers, rub the grass stain with glycerine, leave it to soak in for an hour, then rinse out.

Methylated spirits can be used on other fabrics. Dab on with cotton wool or a soft cloth, then rinse out with warm water.

GRAVY Gravy leaves a grease-based stain, so plunge the garment into cold water to remove the worst effects, then apply dry cleaning fluid. Wash as usual.

INK On a white shirt, try rubbing white toothpaste into the stain with a toothbrush or nailbrush, leave for a few minutes and then rinse out and launder as normal.

Sprinkle salt on fresh ballpoint stains on white material and brush off the salt as it absorbs the ink. Continue to sprinkle salt on the stain until it disappears. This method works well on carpets and the remaining stain should then be tamped with hot milk. Make sure the milk is completely rinsed off and the area treated with carpet shampoo afterwards, or else you will face a new problem—a smelly carpet.

If the stain is not fresh, rub white material with a cut lemon first, then sprinkle with salt and leave for an hour. Wash the garment as usual.

On colored material mix a 50:50 solution of white wine vinegar and water and soak the stain.

Red ink is more troublesome because it spreads very easily, so tamp it very carefully with moist toilet soap, or ammonia. Or alternate these two, sponging them off as you go.

JELLY (JAM) Sticky jelly (jam) makes really garish stains, especially on light-colored clothes. Add two tablespoons of white wine vinegar to one pint of hot water. Dip the stain into this solution, then lay the garment on top of a clean folded towel. Dab at the stain, working in to the center from the edges.

LIPSTICK If you find your best napkins covered with lipstick, rub a little petroleum jelly into the stain before laundering in hot water with enzyme (biological) detergent.

Eucalyptus oil will also remove most lipstick stains, but when you dab it on (and this applies to the petroleum jelly cure too) be very careful not to smear the lipstick and spread the stain.

Sponge the lipstick stain with a mix of baking soda and lemon juice before washing as normal.

MILK Soak milk stains in a solution of warm water and glycerine. Brush the fabric gently then wash as normal.

MUD Allow to dry and then brush off the excess with a stiff brush. Soak the garment in cold water and rub the muddy part to remove the worst of it. Wash as normal.

Try rubbing a potato on really stubborn muddy stains. Cut a potato in half and rub it on the affected area. Soak it in cool water and then launder as usual.

OIL Try this when you encounter jeans streaked with black bike oil in the washing pile! Oil stains should be treated in a similar way to those from tar. Dab on some eucalyptus oil and leave to soak for an hour to break down the mark, then wash the affected area with soap and water. You should be able to scrub the stain out of the garment.

RUST Cover rust stains with salt and moisten slightly with lemon juice. Leave for half an hour and then wash in a weak solution (a couple of drops in a pint of water) of ammonia before laundering.

SWEAT Sponge white wine vinegar into the stain and rinse before laundering using an enzyme (biological) detergent and the hottest water safe for the fabric. Alternatively make a paste of cream of tartar, three crushed aspirins and warm water. Apply to the stain and leave for 20 minutes before rinsing off and laundering as usual.

TAR In hot weather, tar can fix itself to the most unlikely places. Scrape the excess of your clothes and then rub the rest with eucalyptus oil applied on a cotton wool ball. Make sure you don't spread the mark by working from the outside of the stain to the center, and turn the cotton ball frequently—use more than one if necessary. This should remove the worst of the mark, but if any remains, treat with dry cleaning fluid.

TEA (SEE ALSO COFFEE) Fresh tea stains can be removed by soaking the garment in warm water and a little borax. Soak a blanket's dried tea stain in a solution of one part glycerine and two parts water for 20 minutes. Wash as normal.

TOMATO Soak a tomato stain in tepid water that contains a couple of drops of household ammonia. Alternatively, you can rub a generous amount of foaming shaving cream into the stain, rinse and wash as usual.

URINE Soak the garment in a solution of one part hydrogen peroxide to six parts cold water with the addition of a couple of drops of ammonia. Leave for an hour, then wash as usual.

VOMIT Treat as for feces.

WINE STAINS Everyone has their favorite method of dealing with red wine spills. Here are some of the most popular, but they come with no guarantees! It is hard to predict how different fabrics react to red wine, and indeed, the strength of the stain produced by different wines. In all cases, mop up the worst of the red wine spill with napkins or absorbant cloths before you begin treatment. Act quickly, because the longer the stain lingers, the harder it will be to treat.

The most common (and most wasteful) is to pour white wine on to the red wine spillage. This will certainly dilute the red dyes, but you may not want to waste your finest Sancerre on cleaning the carpet/sofa/guest. Allow the white wine to soak in, then rinse the stain out with lukewarm water.

To remove wine from clothing, use a disposable disinfectant kitchen wipe to absorb the spill. Disposable cloths do not contain so much bleach that your clothes will be marked by the cleaning agents, but if you are concerned about your clothes, you may prefer a different method.

Soda water. Spray or pour a liberal amount on the red wine spillage. The soda water will dilute and neutralize the red wine. Leave the soda water for 10–15 minutes, then rinse it out or mop it up.

Salt. Many people swear by this. Simply sprinkle a liberal amount of salt over the stain, leave for about a half hour to allow the salt to absorb the stain, then vacuum up the salt, and, with any luck the stain too.

Water. This may work especially well on clothes. Simply take the garment and rinse in cold running water, rubbing the stain to remove it.

Old stains. These are the toughest to remove, but try dampening them with white wine before laundering. Alternatively, soak the stain in a glycerine solution for several hours before washing the item.

Drastic action. If the stain has become a permanent fixture on your finest white linen, mix up a solution of equal parts water and hydrogen peroxide and apply to the fabric with a cloth or sponge. As soon as the stain has disappeared, rinse the whole item thoroughly.

TRICKS OF THE TRADE

Avoid ironing by using steam power. Many items will lose their creases if hung in a steamy bathroom. This works best on silk and velvet, as well as other delicate fabrics.

To clean baseball hats without destroying their shape, put them in the top rack of the dishwasher. They will emerge fresh and clean and can be hung by the peak to dry out.

When you get a new shirt, dab the button thread with clear nail varnish to strengthen it and postpone the day when the buttons pop off.

When drying woolen items on a washing line, thread an item of under-clothing through the sleeves and attach the pegs to this. This will prevent unsightly dents which may misshape the sweater when dry.

Rub a greasy collar or cuffs with ordinary chalk. Leave overnight then wash as usual and the mark will disappear.

Remove the residue left by sticky adhesive labels such as price tags by sprinkling the offending mark with a little talcum powder. Wipe with a dry cloth and the adhesive (and talc) will disappear.

HEALTH & BEAUTY

Looking good takes a little bit of extra time, but repays itself in spades. If you feel good, you are more capable of dealing with everything that life throws at you. One famous beauty magnate remarked that there are no ugly women, only lazy ones and she had a point. Today the same applies to men, too. Nobody really has an excuse not to keep themselves washed and scrubbed every day and that is half the battle. Nothing can compensate for the effects of too many late nights and over-indulgence in food and drink, however, so if you really want to look your best.

- Eat a balanced diet at regular mealtimes.
- Drink eight glasses of water every day to keep your body properly hydrated.
- Do not smoke. Smoking dries the skin and promotes deeper wrinkles, quite apart from the appaling effects it has on your lungs.
- Drink alcohol only in moderation.

☞ Exercise (at least go for a walk) every day.

☞ Try to get seven or eight hours sleep every night.

BEDTIME TIPS FOR INSOMNIA SUFFERERS

Another important element in how you feel and look is rest. If you sleep badly you naturally feel less fresh the next day. Make a conscious effort to relax and wind down about an hour before you go to bed. Do not have a large alcoholic drink, as alcohol is a stimulant, and may leave you with a sore head. Nor are sleeping pills a long term remedy. Instead, have a warm bath and perhaps a cup of cocoa—these are old remedies, but proven ones! If you feel you need something more, try these cures for insomnia.

☞ Make sure that you get plenty of exercise, preferably outside. If you are physically tired, you are more likely to drop off to sleep easily.

☞ If you cannot sleep, try elevating the feet by putting them on a couple of pillows or elevating the mattress. This will encourage blood flow back up towards the heart.

☞ Aromatherapists recommend lavender oil for relaxation, so try putting a couple of drops on your pillow. Alternatively, add some lavender oil to a warm bath to really benefit from the fragrant fumes.

☞ Turn the lights down low an hour or so before you go to bed, to lull your body into sleep mode.

☞ You will not sleep well if you are hungry, thirsty, or alternatively, suffering from indigestion after an evening of over-indulgence, so if you really want a good night's sleep, look after yourself in the evening. Follow the old adage of moderation in all things.

☞ One old folk remedy advocates eating a whole boiled onion at bedtime.

☞ Try munching on a banana and a slice of wholemeal toast. Bananas contain the amino acid tryptophan which manufactures serotonin, the neurotransmitter which governs sleep patterns; if you have a low level of serotonin you may well suffer from disturbed sleep patterns. The carbohydrates in the toast help the body to absorb trytophan, and at least it fills an empty stomach.

☞ Another bedtime snack could involve lettuce, which contains calcium, magnesium, and vitamins B3 and B6, all of which soothe the nervous system and relax the body.

Of course, getting to sleep might not be the problem. Many people wake in the night, some of them troubled by a snoring partner. Cures for snoring are many and varied, but the best is probably to move to another bed! Snoring usually occurs when someone is lying on their back, so try to turn the snorer on to their side. Or, if you feel you need a desperate remedy, try sewing a cotton reel to the back of the snorer's pajamas. This will probably stop them lying on their back and they will roll over.

SKIN CARE

It may or may not be true that beauty is only skin deep, but one thing is certain: you must know what type of skin you have before you can look after it properly. Does your face tend to be dry or slightly oily, especially around the "t-zone" of the forehead, nose and chin? Remember that your skin will alter as you age—the oiliness of the teenage years often gives way to dryer skin in middle age. Hormonal, dietary, and environmental changes affect the skin and it often becomes drier and more sensitive with the passing years. Three simple ways to take care of your skin are:

- ☞ Eat a balanced diet, with plenty of fresh fruit and vegetables. Drink eight glasses of water a day.
- ☞ Follow a daily regime of cleaning and moisturizing your skin.
- ☞ Try to exercise. This will improve the supply of oxygen and blood to your skin, helping to keep it supple and healthy.

It is easy to gauge your skin type. Simply wash your face thoroughly and pat dry. After a couple of hours, press a tissue against your face: if it comes away looking slightly greasy, you have oily skin; oil may be present on the part that was in contact with the chin and forehead, which indicates combination skin; and if the tissue is clean, you have so-called normal skin. If your face simply feels taut after washing and drying, your skin is dry. This knowledge will help you to care for your skin properly.

A simple daily routine should involve cleansing, toning, and moisturizing every night and morning to rid your face of dead cells and remove the effects of make-up and pollution. Moisturizing becomes more important as we age, but it is never too early to start! It helps preserve the natural moisture of the skin by forming a protective film over it, and will make your skin feel silky and smooth.

Whatever your daily skincare routine, make sure that:

- ☞ You treat the area around the eyes very gently. This is where the skin is most delicate and sensitive.
- ☞ Avoid pulling or dragging your skin.
- ☞ Use your index finger to apply creams and make-up. Your forefinger is the strongest and usually the grimiest finger as it is used most.
- ☞ Always remove make-up before going to bed, whatever the hour and whatever state you're in! Make-up which is left on the skin for too long clogs pores.
- ☞ Don't forget your neck! The skin on your neck is as sensitive as that on your face, so needs regular moisturizing. One old adage states that you can always tell a person's true age by looking at their neck!
- ☞ Drink plenty of water throughout the day. This has the dual effect of keeping the whole body's moisture levels topped up, and of helping to flush out impurities.

☞ Smoking speeds up the ageing process by drying out skin and deepening wrinkles, so if you really care about the way you look, give up.

SAVE TIME & MONEY

Skin care preparations that promise eternal youth, or at least, firm young-looking skin, are almost as old as time. Today, there are thousands available and it is possible to spend a small fortune in search of that elusive, yet perfect cream. It is not necessary to spend a great deal of money, however. You can use natural ingredients for your own skin care regime, but bear in mind that freshness is all, and you will have to concoct small amounts every few days, rather than large amounts every few months. If you don't want to go to the bother of making your own creams, remember that expensive skin care products are made up of a few basic ingredients and it is possible to replicate their work for a fraction of the cost by using cheaper alternatives. The following tips are inexpensive and worth a try:

Cut a lemon wedge and hold directly on an age spot for ten minutes. Rinse with warm water. Repeat this step every day until the spots lighten or vanish altogether.

A cheap and safe alternative to popping pimples (that inevitably leads to scarring) is to soak a cotton ball in warm salt water and hold it on the blemish for three to four minutes; the nasty white part will dissolve.

This exfoliating scrub will leave your skin soft and glowing. Mix the juice from one lemon with two parts coarse salt and one part olive oil to make a paste. Step into the shower and massage into body. Turn on the shower and rinse. Pat dry and apply a rich moisturizer.

Cut a grape in half and gently crush it on your face and neck. Leave it on for 20 minutes or so and rinse with tepid water and pat dry. Repeat every day and before you know it, supposedly, those wrinkles will be harder to find.

Before bed apply unscented castor oil around your eyes. Remember to cleanse and moisturize your skin in the morning.

To prevent a shiny face, brush your skin, using a clean makeup brush, with pure lemon juice. Let it stand for five minutes then rinse. Do this in the evening before bed since the citric acid may cause temporary redness. Lemon juice contains astringent and antiseptic properties that will get rid of the excess perspiration and unwanted shine resulting from high humidity.

In a cup, combine 10 drops of lemon juice with one half cup of water. Saturate a cotton ball with mixture and dab over clean skin. Do not rinse from the skin.

For under eye circles and wrinkles, mix a drop or two of honey with two to three drops of fresh lemon juice. Apply to the area under the eye. Leave it on for about 15 minutes to half an hour and it seems to work.

Buy a clean unused toothbrush and apply a dab or two of petroleum jelly to it. Brush lips gently until the dead skin is scrubbed off and rinse with warm water.

Pour a spoonful of honey into the palm of your hand, add three to four spoons of sugar. Massage well into your hands for a few minutes. Rinse and apply hand lotion. Your hands will be silky soft.

Mix two tablespoons of petroleum jelly with the contents of a vitamin E capsule and massage all over your legs. Slip on cotton sweats and go to bed. In the morning, wash your legs with a moisturizing body wash and apply a body lotion. This will soften the skin.

Pour a cup or more of powdered milk into running bath water. The lactic acid in the milk will remove dry dead skin and leave it baby-soft.

Mix one half cup of honey with one half cup of orange juice and apply to the oily areas of skin. Let it sit for five minutes then rinse. Honey heals and banishes blemishes and the orange juice will dry up the excess oils.

For a great deep cleansing scrub, mix four tablespoons of plain yogurt with two tablespoons of grated orange peel. Massage into skin for three minutes. Rinse with warm water. The yogurt is an exfoliant and the orange peel will extract dirt and oils.

To remove the discoloration from your elbows, just cut a lemon in half and rest an elbow in each half for 10 minutes. The acid in the lemon juice breaks down the dark patches, so they wash away.

To relieve dry patches, massage in vegetable oil. It is full of vitamins and replenishing oils and is preservative- and fragrance-free.

After applying make-up, spray mineral water on your face and let it dry. Do not wipe. Make-up will stay looking fresh longer.

An alternative make-up remover is almond or sesame oil applied to the face on a cotton ball. It will even take off waterproof mascara.

To seal eyeliner in place, trace over the line with a powder shadow in a matching shade. Another good tip is to use a fine brush, dip it in water then your powdered shadow, and then trace over your liner.

Petroleum jelly is an excellent make-up remover. It can also be used as a moisturizer. Before bed, smooth petroleum jelly all over your face and leave on for ten minutes before wiping off. Your skin may look a little shiny, but it will feel really soft.

If you have run out of skin cleanser, use cold milk to remove makeup. It is a gentle, yet effective cleansing agent.

If you suffer from acne or oily skin, splash your face with a preparation of equal parts warm water and cider vinegar, and allow to dry without a towel. This helps to restore the natural pH balance of the skin.

Exfoliation invigorates the body and livens up tired skin. Mix up a cup of sea salt with enough warm water to make a paste and use a face cloth to rub the mixture all over the body. Pay special attention to thighs and other areas at risk from cellulite. Rinse off in a warm shower, and moisturize afterward.

As they get older, many women accumulate cellulite on their hips and thighs. There is no easy way to get rid of it, but it can be reduced by exercise and massage. Or you could just use a rolling pin. Roll it over each thigh for three minutes each side before a bath, and it will help to reduce the slightly pockmarked look of the skin.

HOMEMADE FACIALS

A beaten egg white makes an excellent face mask. Beat until frothy, then massage all over the face. Leave until dry, then rinse off with warm water. If you have slightly dry skin, add a teaspoon of honey.

A steam face bath will remove impurities from your skin. Add boiling water to a bowl, and add a couple of drops of lemon juice and a few mint leaves. Cover your head with a towel and lean over the steamy bowl, inhaling the fragrant vapors for five minutes if you have oily skin, two minutes if your skin is drier. Your pores will open up in the steam, allowing impurities to sweat out. Afterwards splash the face with cold water to close the pores and then moisturize as usual.

Cucumber and yogurt can be mashed together to make a reviving face mask. Spread the mixture over your face and leave for about 15 minutes. The two ingredients are a perfect combination: cucumber tones the skin, while yogurt revives tired skin.

An oatmeal face pack will cleanse the skin and slough off dead cells. Mix together one tablespoon of oatmeal with lemon juice to make a smooth paste. After washing your face, apply the mixture and leave for 10 to 15 minutes before rinsing off with cool water.

Relax your eyes and tighten up under-eye bags by resting with a couple of cold, damp tea bags over each eye. After 10 minutes remove them and splash your eyes with cold water to feel really invigorated.

You can achieve the same effect by using slices of cucumber, which are excellent for soothing puffy eyes.

When you use toner, apply it to wet cotton wool. If the cotton wool is dry, it absorbs most of the toner, leaving little to go on your face.

Hair care

Everyone suffers from "bad hair" days now and then, as hormones and pollution in the environment combine to ruin our crowning glories. Wash your hair as often as you feel you need, but if you wash it every day, use a mild shampoo. Frequent shampooing strips the natural oils from the hair leaving it dull and lifeless, so make sure you condition it regularly as well.

Make your conditioner work by leaving it on your head for 20 minutes before rinsing it off.

Cold tea makes an excellent after-shampoo rinse. It makes your hair shine and feel really soft. Massage it into your scalp before rinsing off.

Treat dandruff by mixing up equal quantities of cider vinegar and warm water and apply to the scalp daily.

If you hair is lank and lifeless, simply change your shampoo. Over time, shampoo residues build up on your hair, but they can be banished by using a milder or slightly medicated shampoo instead.

Alternatively, try rinsing your hair with white wine vinegar, which will neutralize the alkalis left by shampoo residues. Massage the vinegar into the scalp and all over the hair, then rinse off.

Body shampoo or shower gel is barely different from hair shampoo. It's also half the price.

If you run out of styling wax use a little petroleum jelly, but don't overdo it. It repels water so will take some time to rinse out.

For that retro sixties beehive, use egg white to hold your hive in place.

If you're expensively tinted blonde hair has gone green in the swimming pool, don't despair. Apply some tomato ketchup and rub well into the hair, then rinse off to restore the color. A less drastic alternative is to rinse your hair in club soda, which should neutralize the chlorine damage.

Olive oil restores lackluster hair and will help tackle dandruff. Give yourself a hot oil treatment by warming a couple of tablespoons of oil in a cup, then rubbing it into your hair. Wrap your head in plastic wrap (clingfilm) and then wrap a warm towel around it and leave for at least 30 minutes before shampooing and rinsing.

Achieve smooth, glossy hair by making sure that the last rinse after shampooing is of a tepid temperature. Cool water encourages the outer cells of the hair to lie flat, thus promoting a silky look.

You can make wax for removing body hair in your own home using just a few simple ingredients. Use one cup of honey, three-quarters of a cup of molasses, half a cup of sugar, and a little juice from a lemon. Heat it until it is just bearable when applied to your skin. Stir, apply to the area you want to wax, and remove the hair and wax by applying strips of linen on top, then ripping them off.

For oily hair, instead of using regular shampoo use lemon dish soap or washing-up liquid. It absorbs all the oil and the lemon also lightens blond hair. Condition the hair afterward.

If you suffer from dry hair, wash it and towel dry, then apply a conditioner of mayonnaise and leave for an hour. Alternatively, whip up an egg white; mix the yolk with one tablespoon of warm water to make a creamy mixture, then combine this with the egg white. Wet your hair with warm water, towel dry, then massage the egg mixture into your hair and scalp. Rinse your hair with cool water. Shampoo with warm water then add a tablespoon of cider vinegar to the final rinse. These ingredients may seem more at home on a crisp green salad, but you will be amazed how effective they are on the condition of your hair.

To get rid of shampoo and conditioner build-up on your hair, take a tablespoon of baking soda and massage it into wet hair, rinse, and shampoo as usual. Do this weekly. For a really great hair cleanser, rinse off the baking soda using a few tablespoons of cider vinegar mixed with warm water.

To get combs and brushes clean, soak in ammonia for a minute or two.

HANDS

Like our facial skin, the skin on our hands becomes drier and more sensitive with age. Care for your hands by:

- ☞ Wearing rubber gloves when doing household chores, and especially when using water and cleaning chemicals.
- ☞ Never wash your hands in really hot water, because it strips the natural oils from the skin.
- ☞ Always apply moisturizing lotion to your hands when you have finished washing up, cleaning, or simply washing your hands.
- ☞ At night, rub your hands with moisturizer and slip on some cotton gloves to really pamper them.

Try rubbing warts with lemon juice twice a day.

Soak chapped hands in warm water mixed with a few drops of essential oil of patchouli or comfrey.

To clean really stubborn stains off your hands, mix up a teaspoon of sugar with a little olive oil and rub all over your hands, working into the stains. Wash off with warm water and soap and apply a good hand cream.

For a really luxurious hand cream, mix together olive oil and petroleum jelly. Rub all over your hands then slip on a couple of freezer bags to let your hands "marinate" and absorb the terrific moisturizing effects.

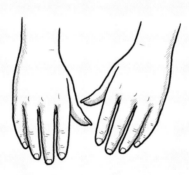

FEET

Don't neglect your hardworking feet. We walk all over them and only really notice them when there is a problem of some sort. It goes without saying that you should change your socks and tights every day to keep your feet fresh. And try not to wear the same shoes every day; let them air properly for 24 hours after a day's use.

This may be obvious, but make sure your shoes fit properly. They should be half an inch (1 cm) longer than your longest toe. Try to wear shoes with leather uppers, which allow the foot to breathe, and manmade soles, which last longer than leather ones. A great many foot problems will simply not occur if you wear properly fitting shoes throughout your life.

Minimize odors from smelly feet by washing and drying them thoroughly every day. If you are prone to sweaty feet, dust them with talcum powder before putting on hosiery. Or try wiping them with surgical spirit, which has a drying effect on the skin.

Try to wear cotton or woolen socks and keep nylon or manmade fibers to a minimum.

Sweaty feet are not an attractive prospect. Try this footbath to reduce foot odor. Pour a quart of boiling water on three teabags and pour this into a footbath. Add enough cold water to make the water a comfortable temperature. Relax and soak your feet for 20 to 30 minutes, then dry your feet thoroughly and apply talcum powder. Repeat every day for a week or so and you will find that foot perspiration is much reduced. The magic ingredient is the tannin in the tea which is a drying agent.

White wine vinegar will help cure fungal nail infections. Simply dab some white wine vinegar on to a cotton wool ball and apply to the affected area twice a day.

If you suffer from athletes' foot, soak your feet in a foot bath made up of equal parts of vinegar and water. The vinegar helps to restore the skin's pH balance and will discourage the formation of foot fungus.

Many people put up with hard and cracked skin on their feet, especially during the summer months. Daily moisturizing with a proprietary foot cream can provide some relief, but make sure that you regularly soak your feet in a bowl of warm water and baking soda to soften the skin, then buff with a pumice stone and apply a really good moisturizer. Afterward, slip on some cotton socks and leave for about 15 minutes to allow the moisturizer to soak into the skin. Better still, moisturize your feet before you go to bed and sleep in socks to get the full benefit.

EXERCISE

We all know that exercise is a good thing, but too many of us do not do enough. Everyone is busy and it is sometimes hard to take time out for a run, some swimming, or even a brisk walk. Doctors are certain, however, that everyone should keep active as it prolongs life, minimizes the chances of ill health, and keeps us mentally alert. Thirty minutes of activity every day also reduces stress. Here are several ways in which you can increase your activity levels without investing in the services of a personal trainer!

Take the stairs, not the elevator.

Instead of using the car for short journeys, walk. Get off the bus a couple of stops before you need to and walk the rest of the way. If you can walk to your local shops, for example, and carry a couple of bags of groceries home, you will combine cardiovascular exercise with a workout for your upper body muscles.

Think of ways to exercise at home. Buy a fitness video, and use it! Or consider installing an exercise bike in the living room, so you can ride while watching your favorite TV shows.

Play with your children or pets. Chase them around the yard or kick a ball around for 15 minutes—it's good for all of you and a lot of fun, too.

If you decide to take the plunge and join a heath club or gym, choose one that is near to your home or place of work, somewhere it is easy for you to visit a few times a week as part of your usual routine.

Minor ailments

There are many folk cures for common ailments like coughs and colds, so if the aspirin or cough medicine aren't working, try some of the following tips.

A throbbing headache can be relieved by rubbing the temples and forehead with a lemon or lime. The aromatic smell is certainly refreshing and will help relieve feelings of fatigue.

Add a few drops of lavender oil to warm water or a fragrancer and inhale the aroma to relieve headaches and migraines.

As soon as an attack of cystitis begins, start a curative regime. Dissolve one teaspoon of baking soda in a glass of hot water and drink it. Repeat every hour for three hours and it will destroy bacteria and reduce inflammation.

If your digestion is troubled by stress or nervous upsets, try drinking a cup of chamomile tea in the morning. Chamomile is an ancient treatment for relaxation, and herbal tea lacks the tannin and caffeine present in normal tea and coffee.

Try other herbal teas, such as marjoram to relieve aching muscles and headaches; peppermint for relief of nauseous symptoms (excellent for women suffering from morning sickness); sage helps to soothe a persistent cough.

Relieve bad breath and neutralize odors such as garlic by chewing on a sprig of parsley. Cardoman pods are also excellent. Chew the whole husk and when it is done, swallow the seeds, and spit out the husk.

Try swallowing a teaspoon of cider vinegar to relieve hiccups. A sweeter alternative is to suck a sugar cube.

Soothe a sore throat by gargling with a glass of warm water (200ml) containing half a teaspoon each of baking soda and salt.

If you have an annoying cough, try to make sure that your home is an even temperature throughout, as moving from a warm room to a cold one can trigger a coughing attack.

Take garlic, either in its raw form or in the form of capsules, to ward off colds and infections. It has natural antiseptic properties and will keep bugs at bay. It is also good for the circulation.

A TOUCH OF THE SUN

Doctors advise us to keep out of the sun as much as possible these days, but nearly everyone suffers from sunburn at some point. Here are a few cures that may be handy if you have mislaid the aftersun lotion.

Grate a raw potato and wrap it in a clean handkerchief or piece of muslin. It will soothe and heal the affected area.

Try spraying the sunburnt parts with vinegar. Add vinegar to a spray bottle and use it to cool burnt bodies.

An alternative is to soak a towel in a solution of cool water and white wine vinegar and drape it over the sunburn victim.

Try to prevent sunburn by following the "slip, slop, slap" regime advocated in Australia:

 Slip on a t-shirt.
 Slop on some suncream.
 Slap on a sun hat.

Stay out of the sun between 11am and 4pm when the sun's rays are at their strongest.

Apply a high factor sunscreen and make sure that you reapply it every couple of hours, especially to children and particularly if you are in and out of the sea or a pool.

Keep to the shade as far as possible.

Drink plenty of water.

Wear sunglasses to prevent squinting in the bright light—it will help in the eternal fight against wrinkles. Many sunglasses protect the skin against sun-damage, so large frames are best.

DEALING WITH MINOR HEALTH PROBLEMS

Accidents happen even in the best regulated households, so it is best to be prepared to deal with them. Minor health problems can be dealt with at home, but more serious and continuing problems need professional help or advice. Below are only suggestions and are not a replacement for a visit to the doctor.

Keep a basic first aid kit to hand and make sure everyone in the family knows where it is (but do not let children play with it.) You can buy prepackaged kits or make up your own. It should contain:

- ☞ Band aids.
- ☞ Antiseptic cream.
- ☞ Antiseptic spray or wipes.
- ☞ Hydrocortisone for treating insect stings.
- ☞ Aspirin or paracetamol.
- ☞ Pain relief for children (if you have any).
- ☞ Absorbent sterile gauze bandages.
- ☞ Adhesive tape.
- ☞ Triangular bandage.

☞ Safety pins to secure bandages.

☞ Scissors to cut gauze and bandages.

☞ Tweezers to extract stings or splinters.

☞ Cotton wool.

☞ Calamine lotion.

It is often hard to assess the severity of an injury, but if in any doubt, get professional medical help.

When cleaning minor cuts and scratches, always wash your hands before and after giving any treatment.

Clean the wound as thoroughly as possible, removing dirt and grit. Use an antiseptic wipe, wet (clean) cloth, or cold running water, which will also slow down the blood flow.

Do not wash or wipe away blood clots as they are signs that bleeding has stopped.

If you get a splinter in your hand, try to remove it with sticky tape before you resort to needles and forceps. Simply apply a small piece of sticky tape over the affected part and rip off. Make

sure you pull off the tape in the right direction—check to see which way
the splinter entered and pull in the opposite direction.

SUBSTITUTES

If you need to administer emergency first aid and do not have the right
equipment, you can improvise using a number of household items.

Clean towels will do as a bandage or pressure pad to staunch bleeding.
If someone is bleeding really badly, don't worry too much about the
cleanliness of the towel; the priority is to stop the blood flow.

Don't use cotton wool or tissue on wounds if possible, as they stick to
the blood.

Sticky tape can substitute for
safety pins.

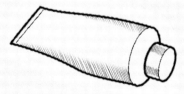

Use frozen peas as an instant ice pack, or a few ice cubes or ice blocks wrapped in a tea towel. Before you apply frozen items to your body, always wrap them in a clean cloth, or they may cause frostbite.

A scarf folded diagonally may be used as an arm sling.

Unlikely as it may sound, rubbing a graze or scrape with the inside of a banana skin not only relieves the burning pain, but also promotes healing.

TRICKS OF THE TRADE

If you run out of shaving lotion, try using peanut butter, which will soften and nourish the skin. Alternatively, rub in some olive oil.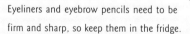

Eyeliners and eyebrow pencils need to be firm and sharp, so keep them in the fridge.

Ensure that your lipstick lasts as long as possible by powdering your lips before applying lipstick.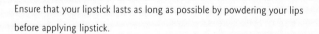

Mend a broken lipstick by melting the broken edges over a candle flame and pushing them together, then smoothing them together with a toothpick. Leave it to set in the refrigerator.

Make your perfume last longer by applying a little petroleum jelly to the skin first. Always apply your fragrance to pulse points and remember that the aroma rises, so the best place for it is the back of the knees!

If you have smudged your mascara while applying it in a hurry, repair the damage by putting a little foundation on a cotton bud and wipe over the excess mascara. Voila, back to square one!

The healthy glow of many celebrities is often due to a dab of colorless lip gloss on their cheek bones. You can achieve this by smiling in the mirror and dabbing some lip gloss onto the fullest part of your cheek and stroking it upwards towards your ear.

Keep your make-up brushes clean to avoid a build up of old make-up and bacteria. Wash them in a mild shampoo and conditioner, then leave them to air dry, preferably hanging them up by the handles.

If you find you are down to the last scrapings from a dry mascara tube, try standing it in a cup of hot water for a minute or two. This will soften the remaining mascara and probably produce enough for a coat or two.

If your hands are really stained (especially with nicotine) try rubbing them with minty toothpaste instead of soap; rinse off and watch the stains disappear.

Cure aching feet by lying down with your feet raised higher than your hips for at lest 15 minutes.

HOME MAINTENANCE

All homeowners will acknowledge that their homes need a little care and attention every now and then to keep things running smoothly. Like cars, houses benefit from an annual service. Jobs like unblocking gullies, clearing leaves, touching up paintwork, leveling uneven paths and other minor repairs are within the capabilities of most people. A little knowledge is often a dangerous thing, but in the area of home maintenance, familiarity with how things work and how to fix them can be extremely helpful.

Even if you are a competent handyperson, and confident of your skills in dealing with gas, water, and electrical concerns, be aware that there are some areas where a licensed and qualified person is the only person for the job. Safety regulations in Britain, for example, state that gas ovens may only be fitted by a registered, qualified fitter. This law, and others like it, is designed to protect the individual, so if you face a problem with a utility service, call in the professionals: safety is a paramount concern in all areas of home maintenance and DIY.

The best way to preserve the investment that is your home is to prepare yourself for the demands of the changing seasons. Make sure the insulation in your home is adequate, that boilers and air-conditioning units are serviced once a year, and that you are generally equipped to tackle minor household problems. Remember, too, that parts of your house will need regular maintenance to stop them falling into a state of disrepair; wooden window frames, doors, fences, and outside walls all need attention such as a coat of paint to preserve them against the elements. Check the fabric of your building one or twice a year to guard against any dilapidation.

BEFORE WINTER GETS AN ICY GRIP:

- Stock up on rock salt to grit icy paths.
- Invest in a shovel to clear snow.
- Make sure that doors and widows are well-fitting to minimize drafts. Consider hanging longer and thicker curtains to improve insulation.

- Check that all pipes are sufficiently lagged to minimize freezing.
- If you have an open fire, get the chimney swept.
- Have the household boiler or furnace serviced. There is nothing more

miserable than a malfunctioning central heating system just as the first big freeze of the season sweeps down from the frozen north!

IN SUMMER:
- ☞ Make sure that windows open properly and can be fixed securely.
- ☞ Ensure that air conditioning units and vents function correctly.
- ☞ Check fly screens for holes.
- ☞ Check brickwork and foundations for cracks.

Domestic disasters afflict us all from time to time, and it is best to be prepared for them. You can significantly minimize the danger to your family and the damage to your home if you know how to turn off the power and water to your house in times of crisis.

Keep a list of the contact details for utility companies—telephone, electricity, gas, and water, as well as plumbers, electricians, and handymen. Make sure everyone in the family knows where the list is kept in case of domestic crisis.

Even more important, familiarize yourself with the fuse box before you

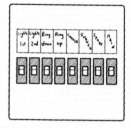

have an electrical blackout. Keep some spare fuses and a torch nearby in case of power cuts or blown fuses.

Find the water main stopcocks and check that you can use them to turn off the main water supply to your house. Check that the main stopcock works and does, indeed, turn off all the water in the house.

Do the same with the gas supply. If you smell gas, check that all the gas appliances are off and immediately alert the gas company. Tell the members of your household and nearby neighbors, open windows, and do not use any naked flames until the problem is resolved.

BASIC TOOLKIT

Have a basic toolkit ready to deal with minor domestic repairs. It should contain:

- ☞ Screwdrivers, both cross-headed and straight-headed,
  or an electric screwdriver
  with a variety of heads.
- ☞ Allen keys.

☞ Hammer with a claw for removing nails.

☞ Tape measure.

☞ Plumber's wrench—a large adjustable spanner.

☞ Small adjustable spanner.

☞ Pliers.

☞ Chisel.

☞ Torch.

☞ Protective goggles.

☞ Electrical tape.

☞ Duct tape.

☞ Small hacksaw.

☞ A selection of nails and screws with wall plugs.

☞ Glue—epoxy resin, PVA, and a rubber-based solution.

It is also sensible to ensure that you have spare light bulbs, candles, and a torch in an easily accessible place.

If you store candles in the freezer, incidentally, they will not drip when lit.

REGULAR MAINTENANCE

Keep extractor fans and vents working smoothly and efficiently by cleaning them regularly. Either brush out dust and grime with a stiff brush, or vacuum the vent to remove a build-up of dust. Kitchen vents will need to be cleaned with hot soapy water to remove grease.

Heaters—of all types—will need similar treatment. Make sure the heater is turned off at the mains, then use a static-attracting duster to vigorously clean out the vents. Follow this by a using the vacuum hose to vacuum out any remaining dirt. This will ensure that when you switch the heater on for the first time, you will not be choked by a cloud of rising dust.

Fit smoke detectors and carbon monoxide detectors to your house. Test them and change the batteries regularly. Carbon monoxide is odorless and invisible, but can be produced by appliances (such as water heaters, cookers, furnaces, and fires) which do not burn their fuel properly, or have blocked chimneys. Vehicle exhausts and portable propane heaters and lamps operating in areas with limited ventilation are also potential sources of carbon monoxide.

Inhalation of carbon monoxide, even for a brief period, can be fatal. So, be safe:

- ☞ Never run your car engine inside the garage.
- ☞ Check household appliances for cracks, leaks, and blockages.
- ☞ Ensure that all fires, stoves and central heating furnaces have adequate ventilation and clear flues.

Check the waterproof seals around baths and sinks for cracks and splits. Replace grout and reseal joins if necessary.

When you buy new electrical items, keep the operating instructions and the manufacturer's details safe; you never know when you may need them again!

If you live in an area which is occasionally threatened by extremes of weather, such as hurricanes, check that outbuildings are as secure as possible, that roofs are firmly attached to sheds, that doors are fixed properly, etc.

MINOR REPAIRS
DRIPS AND BLOCKAGES

Dripping taps can become very irritating. If the plumber finds himself busy elsewhere (and he often is), try tying a piece of string around the end of the faucet. The water will flow silently down the string into the sink. And you can wait for the plumber in peace.

Clear out a blocked sink or bath waste pipe by probing it with a thin flexible plastic rod, such as a curtain rod. This should loosen or shift the blockage, which can then be flushed away by pouring a kettle of boiling water down the pipe, followed by a handful of baking soda.

Keep the kitchen sink clear of blockages by tipping a handful of baking soda down, followed by a cup of vinegar. Leave for one hour, then flush through with plenty of boiling water.

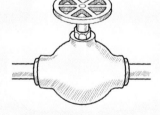

Make a temporary repair to a leaking pipe by first turning off the water supply at the mains, and then drain the hot water tank by turning on all the taps and allowing the water to run out of the system. (Make sure all the basins are clear, with the plugs taken out!) Dry the surface of the pipe thoroughly, and rub the area around the crack or hole with petroleum jelly. Bind it up tightly with a rag or waterproof tape.

STICKS & SQUEAKS

Fix creaking boards by securing the floorboard more tightly to the joist: hammer long floor nails through the board and on to the joist – but watch out for water pipes which may be tracking in the same area!

Another method is blow talcum powder into the crack between the loose boards, which will act as a lubricant and silence the squeaks.

Creaking stairs are also irritating and can be silenced by using PVA (white) glue. Use a chisel to prize a small gap between the board and the riser, then use a piece of cardboard as a spreader to fill the gap with PVA glue.

Use a candle to ease sticky drawers. Rub the end of an old candle along the drawer runners and the drawer itself to grease and lubricate the moving parts.

If kitchen doors snap shut too sharply, fit a square of draft excluder to the inside of the door where it hits the jamb. This will deaden the thud and possibly spare your fingers.

TRICKS OF THE TRADE FOR DIY

Spare your fingers and thumbs when hammering a nail. First push the nail through a piece of stiff paper or card and use this to hold the nail in place while you are working. Just before the nail is finally bashed into place, pull off the supporting paper and hammer the nail home.

Greasing a screw with petroleum jelly will make it easier to screw into wood. The same is true of nails; some carpenters run nails through their hair before using them, utilizing the oil of their hair to lubricate the nail.

If you are trying to insert a screw in an awkward place, put a bit of putty on the screw head. The screwdriver is less likely to slip off and the job will be easier.

If you are trying to clamp two halves of a broken object together while the glue sets, use a drawer to hold everything in place. Put one of the broken halves in a drawer and gently shut it; this leaves both hands free to line up the remaining pieces and stick everything together.

If you need to fill a small hole in a wall, use white toothpaste. Once dry, you can paint over it and no one will ever know!

If you need a plumb line, simply hang a bunch of keys or other suitable object from a piece of string.

Before drilling, make a start hole in the wood or wall by using an awl. The wood is less likely to split and the drill will not slip out of place.

If you need to drill into a ceramic tile, first stick a piece of sticky tape over the tile and drill through that. The drill won't slip and scratch the tile, and the tile itself is then unlikely to crack.

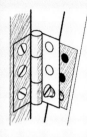

Before you reach for the oil can to silence a squeaky door, try using a little petroleum jelly instead. Unlike oil, it will not trickle down the door frame and on to the floor or carpet.

When hanging a door, insert a wedge or small pile of newspaper under the end farthest from the hinges to support it while you are fixing the screws in place.

Door locks seem to stick for random reasons, but they can be lubricated with a squirt of oil, such as WD40. The lock should then be worked with the key several times to spread the oil through the mechanism.

Another method to tackle a sticking lock is to cover the key with graphite from a pencil, then gently insert it into the lock. The graphite will lubricate the lock system and unlike oil, will not gum up the works.

PAINTING & DECORATING

As with all DIY jobs, check that you have the correct tools and equipment before you embark on a major decorating operation. However impatient you are to give your home a new look, remember that most of your time will be taken up by preparation, so calm your impatience and remember that well-prepared surfaces will look fresh and bright for far longer. No amount of expensive wallpaper or fancy paint effects will disguise a lumpy, pock-marked wall, and gleaming new paintwork never looks good if it is marred by paint dribbles or the remnants of old wallpaper clinging to the wall. This section is not going to include a complete guide to painting and decorating, but a selection of useful hints and tips designed to make the job a bit easier.

PREPARATION

Clear as much furniture from the room as possible and cover the floor with dust sheets or newspaper.

Use masking tape to mask off light fittings, plug sockets, window frames, and skirting boards.

When painting a door, always slide a few sheets of newspaper underneath to catch the drips.

Wear old shoes that you can slip off as you leave the room—you are less likely to spread splotches of paint around the rest of the house.

When filling cracks in the wall, mix the filler with a little of the paint you intend to use. The filler will dry out in the same color as the wall and will be invisible when covered by one more layer of paint.

Cover awkward shapes like radiator heads or taps with aluminum foil or cling film to protect them from paint drips.

If you are painting a ceiling, make a slit in the middle of an old (dry) bath sponge and push the paint brush handle through it. The sponge will catch the drips and prevent paint sliding down your arm or splashing on to your hair and face.

Before you begin a messy job, rub hair conditioner or petroleum jelly over your hands. Dirt and grime will be less likely to cling to your skin and you will find it easier to wash everything off when you have finished your task.

Window cleaning fluid will remove paint from your hands and does not have the pungent smell of white spirit.

Remove the smell of new paint from a room by leaving half a raw onion in the room. Put it on a plate cut-side down and it will gradually absorb most of the paint odors. Replace on a daily basis until the smell has completely disappeared.

If you need to lean a ladder against a wall, avoid marking the wall by slipping a couple of old socks over the ends of the ladder.

Remove masking tape from windows and walls as the paint dries. If you leave it too long, the adhesive will stick to the surface and may mark it.

If you need to remember the position of wall fittings for pictures or lights, stick matchsticks in the holes. If necessary, you can ease the matchstick through the wallpaper—don't worry about the hole, as it will eventually be covered by a fitting.

BRUSHES & PAINT

Always buy natural rather than synthetic brushes as the bristles are less likely to fall out and stick to the wet paint on the wall. Look after your equipment and it will last for years.

If your paintbrushes have become hard and crusty, dip them in a pan of boiling vinegar to soften them up.

Do not throw out used turpentine or brush cleaning fluid. Allow the sediment to settle at the bottom of the jar, then decant the clear liquid and re-use it.

Once you have washed your paintbrushes, rinse them in a little fabric conditioner to keep them soft.

Never store brushes bristle-end down as this will ruin their shape. Instead, put an elastic band around the end of the bristles and store them upright.

If you are going to continue painting the next day, don't bother washing the brushes. Simply wrap plastic wrap (clingfilm) around them or tie a plastic bag around them to keep out the air and prevent the paint from drying and they will be ready for use when you want to start again.

The same applies to paint rollers: just rinse them out and seal them in a plastic bag and they will be ready for use the following day.

Clean brushes without covering your hands in paint by tipping the brush cleaning fluid into a plastic bag, adding the brush, and rubbing the paint out of the bristles through the bag.

Store paint pots upside down (with the lids firmly shut to avoid spillage!) to prevent a skin forming.

Store small amounts of paint in small containers; any amount of air causes paint to dry up.

Label your tins of paint so you can easily see how much you have left by marking the outside of the tin with a line showing the level of the paint left inside.

Professional decorators usually tip their paint from the pot into a smaller container, known as a paint kettle. Line the kettle with aluminum foil and throw this out when you have finished, so that older paint doesn't contaminate newer and different colors when you use it on a later occasion.

When painting stairs, paint alternate treads. Do not tackle the second set of treads until the first set has dried and in this way you will be able to use the stairs (carefully!) throughout the decorating period.

WALLPAPERING

Tie a piece of string across the top of the paste bucket to rest the brush on. It is also useful for scraping excess paste off the brush.

Rinse out pasting brushes in salt water before washing. The brine will dissipate the paste and leave the bristles soft.

If you need to repair a piece of damaged wallpaper, tear a matching piece to cover the hole. Don't cut the paper in straight lines as they will show up far more clearly than irregular ones. Simply match the pattern and paste the patch over the damaged area.

When removing washable or thick wallpaper, scuff the surface with a wire brush or scraper to allow the water to soak in more easily.

Add a tablespoonful of baking soda to each bucket of warm water when stripping wall paper. The baking soda helps loosen and dissolve the paste making the whole job much easier.

Soak old wallpaper by using a paint roller or large sponge dipped in a solution of vinegar and hot water. After two applications the paper should come off the wall effortlessly.

After papering a room, save a little of the wallpaper paste in a screwtop jar, just in case you need a little to stick a stray piece of paper back into place later.

When choosing wallpaper consider these tips:

- A large, bold pattern will make a small room look even more compact.
- Light patterns on a light background will make a room seem more spacious.
- Small random patterns help to disguise lumpy or uneven walls.
- Stripes look best on even walls and are even better when offset by a picture rail or cornice.

SAFETY IN THE HOME

More accidents happen at home than anywhere else, and, according to the Royal Society for the Prevention of Accidents, each year some 4,000 people in Britain die as a result of an accident in the home. Your home can be made safe for the entire family, however, with a little careful thought and planning.

MEDICINES & POISONS Keep all medicines well out of reach of young children, whether in a high cupboard, or in a locked one.

Wherever possible use medicines in child-proof containers.

Never use medicines prescribed for someone else.

Throw away all medicines that are past their sell-by date or any unfinished prescription drugs. Do not throw them in a waste container, but flush them away down the toilet.

Keep all toxic cleaning chemicals in cupboards that are protected by child safety catches. Teach children that they are poisonous and must not be touched.

Make sure that garden pesticides are stored out of reach of both children and animals and always wear rubber gloves when handling pesticides.

GLASS If you have large French windows or patio doors, fix a couple of stickers to them at eye level (adult and child level) to minimize collisions.

Clear up broken glass immediately and wrap well in newspaper before disposing of it. Vacuum the area to remove the almost invisible shards that are inevitably left behind.

If a window is smashed, clear up the glass, then tape cardboard or plywood across the hole with duct tape to keep drafts out.

FIRE If you have an open fireplace, always use a fire guard on open fires and never leave a child unattended in a room with a fire. Consider fixing a nursery fireguard to the wall around the fireplace if you have toddlers.

Keep matches and lighters well out of reach of small children.

Move candles well away from curtains or other combustible materials and never leave them unattended.

Dispose of cigarettes safely and never smoke in bed.

Fit smoke detectors at several points around your house and test them regularly. The battery should be changed twice a year and the alarm should be checked every month.

Do not leave lit barbecues unattended, and always have some water handy nearby.

Consider installing a fire extinguisher in your kitchen.

WATER Never leave small children unattended in the bath. A child can drown in an inch and a half (3 cm) of water. Make sure you have everything you need, such as towels and pajamas, before you run the bath, then you won't be tempted to nip out to fetch something.

If you have a pool or pond, make sure that children are

always supervised in the garden. Teach them not to fool around near the water's edge.

Pools are safer if enclosed by a childproof fence and gate, and all chemicals are stored securely.

ELECTRICITY Keep appliances out of children's reach. Make sure that power cords do not dangle within their reach. If you have pets, tuck power cords out of sight as far as possible to prevent them chewing or pulling on them.

Fit safety covers to all unused power outlets to prevent small children sticking their fingers in them.

Check that all your electrical appliances are in good working order and that none have frayed cables, which are a potential fire hazard.

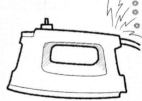

Never run an electrical cord over a hot surface such as a radiator, or under a rug or carpet.

Never leave a hot iron where an animal or small child could pull it over on top of themselves.

Switch everything off at night. To lessen fire risks, unplug all electrical appliances, too.

KITCHEN SAFETY In the kitchen, make sure that saucepans on the hob have their handles turned toward the wall and do not overhang the edge of the stove. It is all too easy to knock a pan off on to the floor.

Always supervise children in the kitchen.

Prevent scalds and burns by keeping the kettle and hot drinks out of the reach of small children. Make sure they are positioned well back on a work surface where there is less danger of them being knocked over.

FALLS Falls are the most common accidents in a house, and usually involve elderly people or young children. Make your house is safe by:

- Installing non-slip flooring.
- Checking that carpets adhere firmly to the floor and that rugs cannot ruck up. Fix them in place with non-skid mesh or padding.

☞ Keep floors, passageways and especially stairs free of objects such a toys which someone may trip over.

☞ Use a rubber mat in the shower or bath.

☞ Check the area outside your house for uneven patches.

☞ In icy weather, grit paths to reduce the chance of slipping on ice.

☞ Make sure that very young children cannot fall out of their cots, high chairs, or buggies. They should be firmly strapped in and someone should be with them at all times.

AROUND THE HOME Remove any small ornaments or objects that are small enough to be swallowed by a child. These include marbles, peanuts, and small toys.

Although most carrier bags these days have a few small holes punched in the bottom, make sure that plastic bags and plastic film are inaccessible to young children; suffocation can result if they put a bag over their head or suck in some plastic.

Unplug electrical appliances that are not in use.

Lock away dangerous implements such as large knives, axes, and firearms. Teach your children never to touch a gun and to tell an adult immediately if they find one.

GARDEN SAFETY Fences and gates should be well made and fitted with locks so that small children and pets cannot squeeze through and get on to the street.

Water butts, ponds, and swimming pools should be securely covered or rendered inaccessible to animals and small children. Do not leave an empty paddling pool to gather rainwater, as it will not take long before it fills up. Small children are almost always fascinated by water, so never leave them unsupervised if there is any danger that they could fall in.

Store and secure ladders so that they are inaccessible to children (and intruders).

Teach children not to eat any parts of plants and not to suck their fingers after touching them.

Make sure that swings and slides are firmly fixed to the ground and site them on grass rather than on concrete.

When using electrical items in the garden, always use a circuit breaker (also known as residual current breakers or earth leakage circuit breakers). It is sensitive to any unusual change in the current and will cut the power instantly. Never use electrical appliances outdoors in the rain or if the ground is wet.

HOME SECURITY

There are a variety of ways in which you can make your house more secure and protect yourself from break-ins and burglaries. Insurance companies, the police, and lock and alarm manufacturers are all additional sources for security advice.

If possible, cover the approaches, path, and driveway of your house in gravel. Burglars prefer a quieter approach to their targets.

If you live alone, consider getting a dog, both as a companion and as a guard. The barking of even a small dog is enough to deter many intruders. If you don't want a dog, leave a dog bowl near the back door to trick burglars into thinking there may be a dog inside.

Burglar alarms are excellent deterrents, but they are expensive. Buy a dummy box and install it on a prominent part of your property to put off potential trespassers.

Install security lights that are sensitive to movement and will illuminate the approaches to your house. Make sure they do not shine directly into yours or your neighbors' windows, however!

Fit window locks to all ground floor windows—at least—and consider fixing them to upper floors and skylights. Although window locks provide extra security, if an intruder really wants to gain entry, he will remove the glass. The only real security for ground floor windows is to fit shutters or a sliding metal grille.

Keep outhouses, sheds, and garages locked. This will not only protect the contents, but also means that a criminal will not be able to utilize the contents (tools and ladders) to gain access to your property.

Lock outside gates to prevent potential criminals "casing the joint."

Although it is convenient to hang keys together in an accessible place, if a burglar were to intrude, he would have instant access not only to your house and its contents, but also to your car and locked sheds or garages as well. So consider keeping keys in a drawer out of sight.

Mark your front door key with a little luminous paint or ink. This will make it stand out from your other keys in the dark and save you fumbling round on a cold doorstep trying to find the correct key.

Never leave a key to your house outside in a "cunning" hiding place. If you are afraid of being locked out, ask a neighbor to look after a key.

Hide your jewelry in the freezer! Simply put small items in an ice cube tray, cover with water and freeze.

Observe your home from outside on a normal evening and note how many lights are on, whether the curtains are drawn, etc. This is how your house should look when you are out. If you are simply going out for the evening, don't just leave the porch light on—switch on a few more around the house.

If you are going to be away, follow these tips to improve home security:

☞ Use a timer to switch lights on at dusk.

☞ Ask a neighbor to open and shut curtains if you are away for an extended period, and to remove mail and post from the door or letterbox. If this is not possible, leave curtains open and ask the mail service to store your mail while you are away.

☞ Leave a radio on so that the house seems occupied.

☞ Make sure valuables are not visible through windows.

☞ Best of all, ask a friend to visit and "house-sit" while you are away.

GREEN TIPS

In Britain each household throws out over one ton of waste each year, yet at least 80 percent could be recycled in some way. In the USA, three-quarters of a ton is produced for each person.

Most of this waste (over 70 percent in the USA) ends up in landfill sites, where it will sit and fester for centuries, much of it breaking down into poisonous compounds. What will this do to the Earth of our descendants, we may ask?

It is better for everyone if we can recycle more of our waste. Many local authorities now encourage residents to recycle a large proportion of their household waste and provide a variety of bags and containers to make the whole process easier. Some families have succeeded in reducing their waste by 50 percent. However, there is no getting away from the fact that bottles, cans, plastic containers, and old papers are bulky items. A little organization, however, will make storing and sorting them until collection day much easier. Don't dump all your recycling in one bag or box—sort it as you go. Designate a bag or box for plastic, another for cans, one for glass, and one for paper.

RE-USE AND RECYCLE

Make sure everyone in the household understands how waste must be disposed of.

Rinse out food containers with your washing up to prevent unpleasant stickiness or odors.

Compress plastic bottles by rinsing them in a little warm water—this will enable you to squash the bottle completely flat.

Some milk cartons and cardboard juice containers with plasticized linings cannot be recycled, but they can be cut up into plant markers and used in the garden or window boxes. Use a permanent marker to write the name of the plant.

If you have a garden, make room for a compost heap and feed it with garden cuttings, vegetable peelings, egg shells, newspaper, in fact anything that is organic and can be broken down. Do not add meat or leftover food as this will attract vermin and smell appaling.

If you have a container for compostable materials (cardboard, garden waste, vegetable peelings, etc,) line the bottom with newspaper which will prevent the organic matter (particularly grass cuttings) from sticking to the bottom and deteriorating into unpleasant green slime!

If you really want to save money, use supermarket carrier bags for your (non-recyclable) waste rather than black plastic sacks. Save your supermarket carrier bags and re-use them when you go shopping. Keep a supply in the car so they will be ready for your next shopping trip.

Cereal bags are usually thrown away, but if you shake out the crumbs, they are useful to cover steaks or chicken breasts when you hammer them to thin them out or soften them.

Save old toothbrushes for cleaning jewelry or scrubbing the grouting in the bathroom. But make sure you keep them away from your current brushes, or you might end up with more than just a nasty taste in your mouth!

When shopping, try to buy products with minimal packaging. Some products are available in "refill" flexible pouches rather than plastic bottles. Keep the original bottle and refill from the pouch.

Use rechargable batteries instead of disposables. As waste, batteries corrode and leak toxic chemicals into the earth.

If you have babies, consider using cloth diapers (nappies) and save the disposables for when you're traveling or away from home. Whatever the argument about energy spent in laundry versus energy spent in manufacturing, in the end, cloth nappies do not clog up landfill waste sites.

Recycling is not just environmentally friendly—it can also save you money. If you are redecorating your house or need new furniture, think about using reclaimed items. Floor boards are a perfect example: reclaimed floorboards look wonderful and lend a great deal more character to a house than laminate flooring or new boards. If you are prepared to strip them and varnish them yourself, you will save even more!

Old furniture can also be painted, stripped, or varnished to suit your tastes and budget. Again, older pieces are often more solid and good looking than many modern flat-pack equivalents.

Check out thrift shops, garage sales, and charity stores for hidden furniture gems. Look for old doors, chairs, tables, bikes (in fact almost anything) at your local tip or reclamation yard. Many people dump perfectly serviceable items simply because they have no room, or they are moving house.

Old floor boards or interior architectural features occasionally appear in builders' skips at the roadside. This is less common than a few years ago, but many people have stories about finding their Victorian fireplace, for example, in a skip.

ENERGY SAVING TIPS

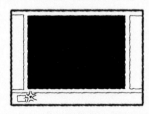

The problems of global warming, air pollution, and acid rain are direct results of the burning of fossil fuels. Reduce fuel consumption and save energy within the home almost effortlessly by switching off unnecessary lights and electrical appliances. It is sometimes hard to relate such small individual actions to the global need to reduce humankind's drain on natural fuel sources, and if you find this concept too mind-boggling, just remember that saving energy within the home ulti-mately saves you money!

When you go to bed, make sure that everything has been turned off. Don't leave computers, TVs and VCRs on stand-by mode, as this wastes more electricity than you realize and is also a potential fire risk.

Do not fill kettles to the brim if you are only making one cup of tea or coffee. Use just as much as you need and the kettle will boil more quickly.

Always use saucepan lids when cooking—the food will heat up more quickly and less energy will be used.

Do you really need to use the car for short journeys? Walk to the local shops or to school to pick up the kids. It's much healthier and will cut down on your petrol costs.

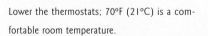

Lower the thermostats; 70°F (21°C) is a com-fortable room temperature.

Use a timer to switch on your water heater for an hour or so twice a day, in the morning and early evening. Chances are that it will store enough hot water for use throughout the day.

Use long-life light bulbs which use 80 percent less energy than regular bulbs, or switch to compact fluorescent bulbs.

Save water by taking showers instead of baths. Don't run water unnecessarily while brushing teeth, washing, or shaving.

STAY COOL IN THE SUMMER

Use heat-producing household appliances like washing machines and ovens in the morning.

Use fans rather than air conditioners.

If you must use the air con, replace air conditioner filters regularly so that the unit runs more efficiently, and switch it off or to about 80°F (26°C) when you are out.

Paint your house a light color. Dark-colored homes absorb more heat that light ones and this results in raised temperatures inside the house.

Plant a tree or two. If you have space to plant a couple of trees on the south or western side of your house, the shade they provide will help keep your home cool.

Close drapes and blinds during the day to keep the house cool.

KEEP WARM IN THE WINTER

Fix radiator foil behind your radiators to save up to 15 percent on your heating costs.

Leave a shallow bowl of water near a radiator to increase the humidity in a room. A warm, humid atmosphere is far cozier and you will be less inclined to turn up the thermostat on the central heating.

Lag water pipes and your water tank to prevent heat loss.

Check that your loft or attic is properly insulated. Increasing the insulation can cut down your heating bills dramatically.

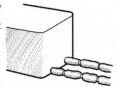

Make good use of your drapes and blinds. Close them in winter to provide insulation and to banish drafts.

APPLIANCES

When using household appliances more is usually less, by which I mean that it is more energy-efficient to put a full load of washing in the machine or dryer than running a half-empty machine. Keep your machines clean and well-maintained and they should run without a problem for many years.

Check the energy rating sticker when buying new appliances which has useful information about the energy usage of a machine. In the USA, look for products with the Energy Star rating —this is the government's seal of approval used to identify energy-efficient appliances.

A similar system operates in Britain and Europe, where the more stars on the label, the more efficient the machine, meaning that it uses less energy than similar-sized machines. Washing machines, for example, not only have ratings for electricity usage, but also for the amount of water they need.

REFRIGERATORS

Place away from natural sunlight and heat-producing appliances. If yours is next to the oven, try to move it!

If you have the space, try to arrange a "cool room," an area of the home where you can safely store fresh foodstuffs without resorting to a powered refrigerator.

The most energy-efficient style of refrigerator is one with a freezer located below the refrigerator space.

Check the seals on fridges and freezers by placing a piece of paper between the seal and the door. If it slides down easily, the door seal is loose or perished and must be replaced. A loose seal means that that fridge is not functioning efficiently or safely.

DISHWASHERS

Maintain regularly to keep then running smoothly. Clean the filters every couple of days to remove debris, and wipe down the door seals to keep them clean.

Read the manufacturer's instructions—an obvious tip, but an important one—as it will mean you get the most from your machine.

It is cheaper, easier, and quicker to wash a few items by hand rather than turn on the dishwasher just for a couple of plates.

WASHING MACHINES

Do not run when only half full, and conversely, do not overload.

Select the correct wash program for the contents of the wash. Do not bother with a really long hot wash for items that are not heavily soiled, for example.

Pre-soak heavily soiled clothes before putting them in the machine and try to operate it at lower temperatures.

Wipe down the door seal from time to time and clean out the detergent dispenser to clear out powder deposits and to prevent mildew forming.

Use a front-loading machine which uses up to a third less water, energy, and detergent than a top-loading model. They also spin more efficiently, leaving you with drier clothes that need less time in the drier or on the line.

TUMBLE DRYER

Do not overload with soaking clothes. Make sure they have been well rinsed by the washing machine first. Follow the manufacturer's instructions with regard to the weight of the load.

Clean the lint filter every time you use the dryer and leave the door open after use to allow air to circulate and any moisture to evaporate.

Make sure the machine is positioned where there is good ventilation to ensure proper circulation of fresh air. Recirculated humid air merely prolongs the drying time.

If you really want to save energy and save money, limit the use of your tumble dryer, and hang your washing on the washing line instead. It's better for the clothes, better for your electricity bill, and better for the environment!

Waste disposal units are pretty much unnecessary if you recycle your organic waste to a compost heap in the garden.

Waste compactors are also becoming redundant as more and more people recycle their cans, bottles, and card. Do not unthinkingly put items into the waste compactor for it all to go on to a landfill site.

COMPUTERS

Do you really need a brand-new super powerful computer? The manufacturing process is not environmentally friendly, using as much in terms of resources as a large car. Consider buying a second-hand machine, which will probably do all the jobs you want, play the same games, and cost a fraction of the price of a new one.

If you decide that your faithful machine really has reached the end of its useful life, do not dispose of it in parts as it may contain hazardous waste; the cathode ray tube from the monitor, for example, contains lead. Recycle the machine via the local solid waste department or local authority environmental services. Or check with the manufacturer which may operate a recycling scheme. Best of all, give it away to someone else—charities, community groups, or even a local child may well be thrilled to receive it.

TRICKS OF THE TRADE

Get a wind-up torch or radio. Not only will you save money in batteries, but they are fun to use, and will work in almost any circumstances—all it takes is a few cranks of the handle to power it up.

Always charge your mobile phone overnight—you may benefit from cheaper electricity rates, and it will be ready for use in the morning.

Many charities or opticians collect old eye-glasses to send to developing countries. Don't throw your specs away, they might be useful to someone else!

Turn items, such as TVs and computers, off when not in use. It is a myth that the small surge of power used when starting up an appliance is anything like as large as the amount of energy used while the device is operating or in stand-by mode.

Make up your own cleaning solutions, which are less toxic and damaging to the environment.

When grocery shopping, avoid shiny fruits as they have probably been coated in pesticides.

Save water when you flush by filling an old soda water bottle with water and putting it in the cistern away from the flush handle. The cistern will use considerably less water, yet will still operate efficiently.

CARS & BIKES

More and more of us rely on our cars everyday to ferry us to work, school, or the shops, and if the trusty family car fails to start, lives are thrown into chaos! Try to keep your car in good working order by having it serviced regularly and by carrying out regular checks at home to keep it in optimum working condition. Make sure you are prepared for the changing demands of the weather and when you leave home on a long journey, always carry a map!

Everyone should be able to look after their car, motorbike, or push bike at a basic level. If you are not confident about getting under the hood of your car, ask a competent friend or relation to take you through the basics. These include:

- ☞ Knowing how to top up the washer bottle.
- ☞ Check the oil level. Oil must be kept topped up in order to lubricate the working parts of the engine.
- ☞ Check the battery connections.
- ☞ Check the spark plug connections.
- ☞ Learn how to check and top up the brake and battery fluid, as well as the radiator.

☞ Find out how to change a tire and use the car jack.

☞ Check tire pressures.

Don't panic if you loose one of the bolts down a drain when changing a tire. You can drive safely for a short distance with three bolts on each wheel, but make sure your first stop is a garage!

If the windshield wiper blade on the driver's side disintegrates, remove the blade from the passenger blade, or use the rear wiper blade until you can make a proper repair.

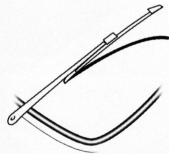

USEFUL THINGS TO KEEP IN YOUR CAR

A disposable camera is very useful if you're involved in an accident. You can take a picture of the accident, photos of the damage to both your car and that of the other party, as well as license plates. Alternatively, it's fantastic to have one on a day out when you find you've forgotten your main camera!

A couple of carrier bags—these are useful for waste, or if a passenger suffers from motion sickness.

Small change for parking, but keep it out of sight in the glove box. If you are a non-smoker, use the ashtray to hide small change for parking.

A demister sponge or cloth for those cold days.

An ice scraper for the windscreen on icy days.

A bottle of water; useful for wiping down sticky children or more obviously, as a drink!

Small packet of tissues for wiping up spills and/or some wet wipes so you can clean your hands after filling up with gas or checking the tires.

A powerful flashlight. If you have one with a flashing feature and a red filter, so much the better. It could be useful in case of an accident or breakdown at night.

At least one, if not two warning triangles.

Maps.

First aid kit.

Fire extinguisher.

Mobile phone. Never use one while driving, but they are invaluable if you are delayed or need to phone for help.

When your car's new, write the license number on a post-it note and stick it on the dashboard until you can remember it.

WINTER TIPS

If you live in a really cold area, do not leave home in winter without a survival pack—a blanket, shovel, and an old mat to put under jammed wheels, and food and drink. Consider taking a flashlight, candles, matches, a battery-powered radio and a small first aid kit. If the weather is really awful, stay at home and wait until the roads are cleared before embarking on a journey.

If you are stuck in your car in snow, don't keep the engine running—you don't know how long you may be trapped and you may run out of fuel. Instead, light two candles, which will provide enough warmth to heat the car interior adequately.

Cover car locks with electrical tape to prevent them freezing.

Frozen locks are often a problem. Never try to force a key into a frozen lock; first, heat the key with a flame from a lighter to warm the metal and allow it to expand. Do this several times, and when you do insert the key, do so gently—a snapped key in a car lock is a nuisance and costly to repair. If you have nothing else, use your gloved hand; leave it over the lock for a minute or two, then swap hands until the metal thaws out. Be aware that in extremely cold conditions metal parts of the car may "burn" your skin.

Use a credit card to scrape the ice of your windshield if you don't have an ice scraper.

Scraping ice off a car is quicker if you have started the engine and warmed the car a little. However, never leave your engine running while you pop inside to collect something—it is all too easy for a thief to take advantage of the situation and drive off in your car.

HOT WEATHER HINTS

In any extreme weather, ask yourself whether the journey is really necessary: a hot, sticky car journey is no fun for anyone. In summer try to travel in the cool of the day or even over night.

Always carry drinking water.

If you have young children, consider fitting a sun blind to the passenger windows to reduce glare and heat.

Never, ever leave young children or animals in a parked car on a hot day. If it really is only for a minute, leave windows slightly open to ventilate the interior.

BATTERY TIPS

If you see you have left your lights on and think your battery may be flat, don't even think about trying to start the car. Instead, turn off the lights and leave the car for at least 15 minutes. If the battery is reasonably strong, it will recharge itself and you will be able to start the vehicle.

To recharge a weak battery, drive around in third gear for a while—the high revs will charge up the battery.

If your car won't start in the cold or damp, spray WD40 on the battery connections.

Avoid problems with damp electrics by parking the front of the car up against a protective wall or hedge overnight.

Avoid gas guzzling

Make sure your tires are inflated to the correct pressure. Under-inflated tires force the engine to work harder which therefore burns more fuel, and the tires themselves will wear out more quickly. Make sure your tires are relatively cool before checking the pressure. Check too that the tread is adequate and that the wheels are correctly aligned. If in doubt, get a qualified mechanic to examine your vehicle.

Observe speed limits for optimum petrol consumption. Drive gently—sudden acceleration and braking is both uncomfortable for passengers and guzzles gas. Try to anticipate the traffic conditions ahead of you and give yourself plenty of time to react.

If you have air conditioning, use it wisely as it burns up fuel, especially in congested traffic.

On highways and motorways, keep your windows closed to minimize air drag.

Remove unnecessary weight from your vehicle and take off the roof rack when you are not using it. Less weight means you will achieve more miles to the gallon and roof bars make a car less aerodynamically efficient.

CAR CLEANING

In winter make sure you clean your car regularly, especially if you have been out in snowy or icy conditions. Mud, salt, and grit on the roads can stick to the car and may corrode some parts, so it is best to visit the car wash from time to time. Make sure the undercarriage is cleaned as this is where the most damage will occur.

Never use liquid soap from the kitchen to clean your car as it contains salt which may encourage the formation of rust on the bodywork.

If you're proud of your chrome wheels, use lemonade to clean them. The shine it produces is magnificent.

Chrome fenders will look super after being rubbed with petrol and then buffed with black boot polish.

Windows polished with newspaper will be sparkling and free of smears.

Baking soda makes an excellent non-toxic cleaner for both the interior and exterior of a car. Use a quarter of a cup of baking soda in a quart of warm water and apply this mild abrasive with a sponge or soft cloth to remove road dirt, bugs, and tar. It will also clean chrome, windows, tires, vinyl seats, and floor mats.

Keep an old toothbrush to clean those tricky inaccessible areas of a car's interior, especially around the gearshift and dashboard.

Remove odors from the car by sprinkling the seats with dried baking soda, and leaving for half an hour, then vacuuming.

After you have washed your car, use your leaf blower to "blow dry" the car and get water out of every nook and cranny.

Carry a microfiber cloth to clean up dust and smudges inside the vehicle.

Try rubbing stubborn sticky marks with a little WD40. This will also help remove melted crayon from the vinyl part of a car interior. Spray on the offending stain and rub off.

Tricks of the trade for cars

If your garage is a rather snug fit for you car, lay down a thick plank against the back wall of the garage. When your wheels hit it, you will know it is time to stop and will avoid scratching your vehicle.

If your garage is poorly lit, paint the walls white, which will maximize the existing light and reflect the beams from your headlamps.

Cut the sleeves off an old shirt and keep them in your car. If you ever have to open the hood or change a tire, slip the sleeves over your arms to protect them from oil and grease.

Car windows often steam up on a cold morning, but you can easily disperse it by smearing a cut potato across the inside of the windshield and wiping off the excess moisture. Rubbing liquid soap across the windshield should do the same job.

Chewing gum will temporarily seal a hole in a leaky radiator.

If your paintwork is scratched, cover the scratch with a little household wax to make it waterproof and to prevent corrosion.

Oil spills on the driveway or in the garage are unsightly. If you suffer an oil leak, tip a generous amount of cat litter over it to absorb the oil. Leave for 24 hours (possibly longer) then sweep up.

If you're about to embark on a messy and oily job, rub your hands with hair conditioner. This will prevent oil adhering to your hands and getting stuck under your fingernails.

MOTORBIKES

The most important thing when riding motorbikes (and the same applies to push bikes) is visibility: it is critical that the rider is visible to other road users. The most common cause of accidents is when car drivers fail to see bikes. So make sure that you always ride with your headlamps on and use high-visibility clothing.

Helmets are required by law in the UK and are mandatory in over half of all U.S. states. They are a biker's best protection against fatal or disabling head injuries, so it is sensible to wear one. Replace them regularly if the finish becomes cracked and never use one that has been involved in an accident.

Do not ride without protective clothing—this is the buffer between your skin and the tarmac in the event of an accident.

Do not take passengers until you are a competent biker and accustomed to riding in different road conditions. Insist that they are properly equipped and know how to ride safely with you.

If a biker has come off his or her bike, never attempt to remove the helmet until paramedics have assessed the injuries. People with back and neck injuries should be moved as little as possible.

If the worst happens and your bike falls over, don't panic—you can right it by yourself if you have the knack. Go round to the front of the bike and grab both handlebars. Lever the front up using both arms, and the rear of the bike should follow.

Like cars, motorbikes suffer from mud and the corrosive effects of grit and salt in cold weather, so clean your bike regularly.

BICYCLES

If you have bikes in your household, it is important that you have the right equipment to keep them running smoothly and safely. Everybody should check their bike before they use it, and children's bikes are especially important, as they often suffer vigorous use from their energetic owners. Over 900 cyclists were killed in the USA in 1999 (according to the National Safety Council), and over 70,000 were injured. Make sure that you are not one of these statistics by following a few safety tips.

BIKE EQUIPMENT

Many people think helmets are unnecessary, citing the fact that they never had one when they were children. But think about how much road traffic has increased in recent years. Head injuries account for 85 percent of cycling related injuries in the USA. Bike helmets save lives, so it is always best to wear one.

Increase your visibility by wearing light-colored clothing, or even better, a fluorescent vest. In Britain it is illegal to ride a bike after dark without ade-  quate lights.

A puncture patch kit, including tire levers (irons) to ease the removal of an inner tube is a necessity. You will also need a pump to reinflate any tires.

A dumbbell spanner will fit a variety of nuts and bolts and a set of Allen keys will always come in handy.

Bikes should be properly secured, even at home. Note down the frame number of your bike and use an ultra violet pen to write your name and contact details on the frame. These will be invisible to thieves, but will show up when a ultraviolet light is shone over them by the police.

THINGS TO CHECK

Tires need to be properly inflated with a tread that is not worn down.
The bike will work more efficiently with pumped-up tires.

The wheels should turn freely.

The brakes should work. Put the brakes on and try to push the bike for-
wards and backwards against them: the bike should not move.

The handlebars and the seat should not be loose and should be at the
correct height for the rider. When you are sitting on the saddle, the balls
of your feet should touch the ground. You will maximize the power of
your bike if it is correctly adjusted to your size.

The chain should be adequately oiled and the pedals should turn freely.

Reflectors and lights should be firmly attached and clean.

The helmet should fit snugly and should not
move if you nod or shake your head.

TRICKS OF THE TRADE FOR BICYCLES

When cycling long distances, remember to wiggle your hands and fingers to prevent numbness.

Wear several layers of clothes, which provide more efficient insulation than one chunky one.

Keep a plastic bag handy and put it over your saddle when you stop on a rainy day. When you return to your bike, you won't suffer the discomfort and indignity of a wet bottom.

Always lock you bike securely in a busy area, and position the lock high in the frame. Thieves who have to bend down to break locks are more inconspicuous.

If you need to mend a puncture and don't have any tire levers, use a couple of old spoons instead.

Use household wax to polish metal and painted surfaces that are prone to rust.

GARDENS & PLANTS

"God almighty first planted a garden, and indeed it is the finest of human pleasures."

Francis Bacon (1561–1626)

There are two schools of thought about gardens: one is that they are places of contemplation and relaxation where one can enjoy being outdoors and simply sit back and bask; the other is that they are a kind of battleground, in which man (or woman) attempts to tame nature and bend it to his or her will. Children, of course, steer a middle course, generally approaching the garden as a place of recreation, tearing over your precious lawn on their bikes and squashing carefully tended plants during vigorous ball games. Whatever your approach, sit back in the lounger and peruse these tips to help you maintain a glorious garden.

TIPS FOR A GORGEOUS GARDEN

Really stunning gardens are those that make the most of the local conditions and work with the local soil type or amount of available shade and light.

Find out what type of soil you have, whether it is acidic or alkaline, a chalky soil or a lime soil, full of clay or slightly sandy. Once you know this you will be able to grow plants which will flourish in the conditions of your garden and will not waste time or money on those unsuited to your soil.

Pay attention to whether plants need a shady or sunny spot; this will have a critical impact on their health.

Get a water butt to store rainwater. It not only saves using domestic water, but rainwater is far better for plants.

Don't throw old string away, but reuse it for tying up plants.

Although it is impossible to make hard and fast rules about the pruning needs of all plants, there is one rule which can be safely applied. If you are unsure about the best time to prune a plant, do it shortly after the last flower fades. Remember the old rhyme for spring pruning, "If it flowers before June, do not prune."

Bury banana skins and crushed egg shells near the roots of your favorite rose bushes to release extra vitamins and minerals into the soil.

Plant garlic near rose bushes to discourage greenfly.

Azaleas and camellias appreciate a little tea! Fertilize them by burying used tea bags around their roots.

Save your nettles to make a fertilizer for tomato plants. Pull up nettles, leave them to rot and then put them in an old bucket and cover with water. Leave for two or three weeks and use the water (which will be rank and strong-smelling) on tomato plants as a fertilizer.

Once you have raked up moss from the lawn, store it somewhere damp and re-use it to line hanging baskets in the spring.

If you are digging a new flower bed and want a curved edge, unroll your hose and drape it around the area that you need. It will make a great marker for you to follow.

Clear up the remains of a bonfire by scattering the ashes on the flower beds. Ashes are an excellent fertilizer and will also discourage beetles and insects.

BUYING PLANTS

It is easy to be overwhelmed by the sheer choice available in a large garden center, but it is easier to choose quality products if you do a little research before you shop. If you have decided on what you want before you get there, you will at least be able to concentrate on the species you need. In general:

☞ Choose plants with an even shape. Plants with trailing, straggly bits or withered leaves are not entirely healthy.

☞ Make sure that the plants have abundant roots and sound stems. If the plant lifts easily out of its pot, avoid it.

☞ Check the compost. It should be just moist like a good cake. If it is dry, the plant may be seriously dehydrated.

☞ Do not automatically choose the plant with the most flowers. Plants in bud are probably a better bet as they will bloom once you have got them home.

☞ Biggest is not always best. Large plants are more expensive, whereas smaller ones are cheaper and probably younger. Younger plants will be easier to establish in your garden, where they will quickly grow to the optimum size.

Buying new plants can be expensive, so why not swap cuttings with other gardeners or neighbors?

TACKLING WEEDS

It is often said that weeds are simply plants in the wrong place (or rather more poetically, "a plant whose virtues have not yet been discovered," according to Ralph Waldo Emerson) and while this may be true, many gardeners take a less tolerant view. The only cure is regular weeding and spraying with a commercial weed killer, but you could try the following tips too.

Try using vinegar as a weed killer. It is a less poisonous treatment than a commercial preparation and will not harm pets if they come into contact with it. Pour undiluted vinegar onto troublesome weeds a couple of times over the course of a week and they should die away, never to reappear. Some gardeners believe that hot vinegar is more effective, but either treatment will make the soil acidic, discouraging weedy growth.

Re-use the salted potato water in which you cooked the spuds to kill weeds on paths and drives.

Use an old potato peeler to dig up weeds, it's just the right shape to deal with tenacious roots.

Dig them out regularly. This is a rather depressing tip, but is really the only sure-fire way to achieve a weed-free flower bed. Do each patch really thoroughly rather than skimming over a larger area.

Use a hoe to rip out young weeds and to preserve your back and knees! The best time is in the morning, as the weeds will then die in the sun. If a bed is completely dominated by invasive weeds, dig out all the plants and wash the roots under running water to remove any traces of weed on the plant roots. Rigorously weed the bed to clear it of all traces of weeds and replace the plants.

Mulching, or covering the earth of the beds around the plants with a thick layer of organic or inorganic material, effectively fertilizes the soil and represses weed growth. Commercial growers often use black plastic, which looks rather nasty, but it is effective and can be covered with a layer of wood chippings or bark to soften the visual effect. Dead leaves, straw, grass cuttings, gravel or simple compost work just as well, although each is suitable for different areas of the garden. Grass cuttings, for example, are better underneath shrubs or bushes, whereas compost works best on flower beds. If applied properly, the thick mulch will block out light and therefore restrict weed growth. Even newspaper can be used as it rots down reasonably quickly and effectively blocks out light to discourage weeds.

LAWNS

Really lush lawns are achieved after years of careful attention and TLC, so be aware that there are few quick fixes for a scrubby patch of grass.

Choosing grass seed and turf should be regarded as a long-term investment. Grass seed is available in many different varieties, so ask at your local garden store for advice about what grows well locally and read the packaging which will probably include plenty of advice about the best type of soil for the particular seed.

When spring arrives and it is time for the first cut of the year, give the lawn a trim, rather than a crew-cut! Keeping the grass reasonably long will protect the turf against late frosts.

Never try to mow the lawn when it is wet. Not only do you risk churning up the turf, but there is also a danger that you will slip and hit the rotor blades.

If you keep your lawn too short, the roots will be shallow and the lawn will be in danger of drying out. Keep your lawn at least two inches long and never cut more than one–third off the length of the grass.

Just-mown lawns look (and smell) wonderful, especially when the stripes left by the mower are still visible. However, it is best to alternate the direction of your mowing each time you do it to encourage the grass to grow evenly. So mow north to south one week, and east to west the following week to prevent the grass from leaning over.

Lawns benefit from infrequent but heavy watering, rather than daily light watering. The average lawn needs to be soaked by about an inch of water a week; this amount will soak down to a depth of four to six inches and irrigate the root system.

If you use a sprinkler system, check its capacity by placing a few old cans around the lawn and switching on for half an hour. Check the level of water in the cans after that time to see how evenly the water is dispersed and how much has been dispensed. This will allow you to work out how long to use the sprinkler to deliver the critical inch of water.

If you leave the clippings on the lawn they will act as a natural source of nutrients. In dry weather they act as a light mulch to conserve moisture in the ground.

WATER

Water is obviously the lifeblood of any garden, but in these days of global warming, even in temperate climates we cannot rely on rainfall as we used to, so gardens must be artificially watered. Lavishing water on your lawn in time of drought is not just a luxurious indulgence, it is a criminal waste. Try some of these tips which will preserve your plants without wasting natural resources.

Get a water butt and install it so that it catches run-off from drains and gullies as well as rainwater. Untreated rainwater is far better for gardens than tap water.

Stop your water butt freezing and splitting in winter by floating a piece of wood in it.

Water the garden in the cool of the day, preferably in the evening when less water will be lost through evaporation and it has more time to soak into the earth.

At the end of a hot day splashing in the yard, don't just tip the children's paddling pool water down the drain—use it on the plants.

Use bath water on the garden in times of water shortage, although avoid water that has had bath foam or oil in it.

The best protection against dry conditions in the garden is to make sure that beds are deeply dug and well supplied with mulch and compost.

Wind dries out plants very effectively, often more than the sun, and if they cannot replace moisture from the soil they will wilt. So, make sure that delicate plants are shielded from the wind behind larger, tougher plants, or garden features.

GARDEN PESTS

There is no better sight than children playing outdoors in the fresh air away from the TV and computer games, but the keen gardener may not welcome their presence in a carefully tended garden. If you have a big enough yard, try to create a section for the children to play in and another in which you can cultivate your favorite plants. If this is not possible, remember that the children will not be boisterous forever, so consider postponing your most extravagant horticultural dreams for a few years until they have outgrown the ballgame phase. (See the section on container gardening for a few tips!)

Animals are no great respecters of herbaceous borders or lawns, and many a gardener has suffered at the hands of a dog determined to dig an escape tunnel. If your dog loves digging, think about providing him with a sandpit and bury a few toys in it. The dog will enjoy unearthing the toys, but don't punish him for digging elsewhere; instead reward him every time he plays in the sandpit and he'll soon stick to that area.

Some gardeners resent the presence of the neighbor's cat in their garden, although it may be doing a valuable job in scaring off other pests such as moles and rodents. However, if you wish to deter feline visitors, remember that cats dislike bright reflective light. Half-fill a few empty soda bottles with water and leave them around the garden where they will catch the light. The glare soon send the cats elsewhere!

Another method is to scatter orange and grapefruit peel around the border as cats hate the smell of citrus fruit.

Cats also dislike pepper, so season the edges of your flower beds with a generous sprinkling.

If you live in a rural area and are troubled by rabbits nibbling away at your plants, try scattering human hair around the base of the plants. Rabbits hate hair and will steer well clear of any plant protected by it. If you don't have enough of your own hair to spare, ask a hairdresser for the sweepings from their salon.

When you have pruned the roses, leave the cuttings on the ground—neither rabbits or cats like a prickly environment.

MOLES

Moles create small volcano-like eruptions across lawns and long tunnels underneath. Most gardeners hate them and there are many vicious traps commercially available in which to catch them. A wide variety of more humane solutions are also available, but are less immediate in effect.

Insert a stick about six inches into the ground near the mole hills, leaving a foot or so poking out above ground. The moles should be deterred by the vibrations created by the wind blowing in the stick.

Similarly, some gardeners advocate planting empty bottles up to their necks in the mole hills or around the garden. The moles will be frightened by the sound of the wind blowing across the tops of the bottles.

Line the bottom of a mole run with gorse or another prickly bush. Moles hate having their noses pricked.

Insert a piece of ground elder into the top of the mole hill.

Moles dislike caster oil, apparently, and many commercial preparations are based on castor oil. Try tipping a slosh of castor oil into the run.

Grow plants that moles dislike, such as caper spurge (*Euphorbia lathyris*), also known as the mole plant or sassy jack. When broken, the leaves emit a bitter milky sap which sensitive moles dislike. (It is mildly toxic if ingested and the sap produces minor irritation if it comes into contact with the skin.) The castor bean or castor oil plant (*Ricinus communis*) has huge star-shaped leaves and is also slightly toxic to humans as well as unpopular with moles.

Pour foul-smelling liquid into the run, such as a weak solution of household ammonia or old cut flower water.

CREEPING & FLYING PESTS

Slugs and snails consume twice their body weight every day, so the potential damage to leafy plants is immense. They can be controlled by slug pellets, but if you are concerned about the adverse the effects these may have on the environment, pets, or small children, try the following remedies instead.

Make a "green" slug trap by leaving some beer in a saucer or small pot sunk into the ground. The slugs will crawl in, slurp some beer and drown. This also works with snails which are similarly greedy little slimeballs and fond of the odd drop of beer.

Mulch the area around leafy plants with broken eggshells or gravel as slugs and snails hate sharp surfaces.

Snails breed in gaps in masonry, so check your house and outbuildings for loose brickwork and fill in the gaps. Obviously this won't wipe out the snails, but it may encourage them to move house!

If snails and slugs are munching on potted plants, smear petroleum jelly around the base of the pot and they will slide away defeated.

If you have access to a ready supply of seaweed, scatter it around your flowerbeds to deter slugs.

Keep slugs and snails away from lettuces by sprinkling soot or coal dust around the plants.

Make up a spray of dilute liquid soap and water to deter insects. Spray on roses to deter greenfly and other bugs.

Another effective home-made spray is garlic tea. Infuse four peeled cloves in a pint of hot water. Leave to stand for half an hour, then spray on the plants.

Young carrots are popular with pests, but they can be protected if they are surrounded by a protective wall of coffee granules.

Protect greenhouse plants from insects by growing a few carnivorous plants (such as Venus flytrap) alongside them.

CONTAINER GARDENING

Anyone can cultivate plants and flowers, even if they are urban apartment dwellers. Window boxes, pots of herbs, and tubs of plants will
liven up your apartment or yard. They are really versatile and their floral
displays can be changed easily to match the passing seasons. Here's
how to keep them looking fresh and healthy.

After a while, container compost will become compacted, and
water will not soak into the soil efficiently, so prick it every
month to aerate the soil.

Make sure that the compost is an inch or two below
the rim of the pot so that soil does not run off when
the pot is watered.

If you are planning to keep your containers on a roof, check
that the building structure is strong enough. A cubic meter of soil
weighs a ton, and the weight will be even greater by the time you have
added pots and plants.

If you are filling a large pot, assemble pot, compost, and plant in the right spot by carrying them separately. Don't pot a large plant and then try to move it—you will likely strain your back!

Clay pots are heavier and more expensive than plastic, but they absorb water and are less likely to become waterlogged.

Remember to protect clay and terracotta pots against frost by standing them on special "pot feet" available at any garden store. Note that some terracotta is not suitable for outside use in winter.

A full hanging basket may be awkward to move into the required position when full, so consider hanging it in place and standing on a ladder to plant it.

Hanging baskets look glorious, especially when hanging at eye-level, but they are awkward to water in this position. It might be worth hanging a basket from a pulley system so that it can be easily lowered for a daily drink.

Hanging baskets tend to drip lots of water, so lessen waste by incorporating some moisture-retaining gel with the compost when planting it.

Use an empty liquid soap bottle to irrigate your hanging basket when you go on vacation. Fill the bottle with water and insert it into the compost, nozzle end down. Water will slowly drip out of the bottle and keep the plants moist.

Remember that freshly watered hanging baskets are heavy, so check that the supports and fixings are strong enough to cope before you position your basket.

Grow basil in the kitchen to deter flies.

GARDEN FURNITURE & TOOLS

Use a paste made from baking soda and water to shift stains on white plastic garden furniture.

Before storing metal garden furniture for the winter, rub down with cooking oil to preserve its shine and to prevent rusting. Polish with a dry cloth before using it again the following spring.

Leave a piece of chalk in your tool box to absorb moisture and avoid rust gathering on your precious tools.

If garden tools have become rusty, mix up two tablespoons of salt with one tablespoon of lemon juice and rub vigorously over the rusty parts.

GARDEN HEALTH & SAFETY

It is easy to relax your vigilance when you are enjoying the garden, but if you have small children, remember that their endless curiosity can sometimes be dangerous. Be aware of their movements around water features, pools and ponds, and check that their admiration of the floral displays does not extend to eating parts of them!

Put soap under your fingers before you begin gardening; there'll be less room for mud and your hands will be easier to clean afterward.

Everyone should wash their hands thoroughly after gardening and particular care should be taken with children who are at more risk of picking up toxocariasis from the larvae of the common dog roundworm. These larvae can live in the soil for several years and are most common in public parks. If you have a dog, be especially cautious and discourage children from hand-to-mouth contact when playing outside or with the family pooch.

Make sure that your tetanus vaccinations are up to date. A bit of dirt or soil in a graze or cut could cause a nasty illness first manifested by an aching back and abdomen and stiffness in the jaw (hence the alternative name of "lockjaw").

INSECT BITES

Usually a painful annoyance, insect bites rarely develop into anything more serious. Be prepared to tackle them with these tips.

Don't panic if a stinging insect lands on you. Do not flap your arms and hands as this is threatening and the insect is more likely to be scared into stinging.

If a wasp lands on someone it is in search of food. Keep still or move slowly in the opposite direction and it will probably fly off once it realizes that you are not a source of water, nectar, pollen, or sugar.

Most people suffer a swollen itchy patch as the result of a bee or wasp sting, which can be treated with antihistamine cream or spray, so keep some in your first aid kit. If someone has been stung more than once or has been stung in the mouth, seek medical help immediately. A mouth sting could lead to a blocked airway, so if possible give the victim ice to suck to minimize swelling.

Soothe a sting by making a cold compress. Dissolve a teaspoon of baking soda in half a pint of water and soak some kitchen towel in the solution. Apply to the affected part.

Flick off bee stings with a finger nail. Do not try to pinch the sting between thumb and forefinger as you are more likely to squeeze the sting (and the remaining venom) deeper into your skin.

Be very careful if you are eating or drinking outdoors. Wasps get very angry if thwarted in their attempts to savor almost any food, fresh or rotting. Keep waste containers well covered in summer to deter them.

If you are enjoying an outdoor drink, always check that it is not harboring a stinging insect and be especially careful with cans of drink.

Wasps are least harmful in the spring when they feed on garden pests such as aphids, greenfly, and blackfly. They become more dangerous in late summer when their diet changes to sweet things.

Make a wasp trap by dropping a teaspoon of jam into a dilute solution of beer. Cover the top of the jar or glass with paper held in place with an elastic band and poke a hole in the middle. The wasps will be lured inside, will be unable to escape and will drown.

Exercise extreme caution when using power tools and mowers. Never leave them switched on and make sure that children and pets are away from the area you are working in.

BRINGING THE OUTSIDE IN

CUT FLOWERS

Pick flowers in the cool of the morning or evening rather than in the heat of the day; they are less likely to be dehydrated.

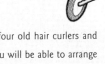

When cutting flowers for an arrangement, make diagonal cuts across the stems and do so under running water so that the water can run into the stem.

Use an elastic band to bind together three or four old hair curlers and stand them upright at the bottom of a vase. You will be able to arrange flowers far more easily with the support of the curlers.

Smash the woody stems of flowers like roses and cut soft stems before arranging your flowers.

Add a teaspoon of bleach to a large vase of flowers to stop the water going cloudy.

If you are arranging flowers with small or broken stems, slide them into drinking straws cut to the required length for the arrangement.

Daffodils last longer by cutting them above the white stem base and by placing a copper coin in the water in the vase.

Prolong the life of cut flowers by misting with a gentle application of hair spray. Spray the underside of leaves and petals from a distance of 12 inches (30cm).

HOUSE PLANTS

When buying house plants look for:

- ☞ Firm healthy buds.
- ☞ Unspoilt flowers. Any sign of browning or wilting suggests that the plant lacks nourishment.
- ☞ Strong, well-colored foliage without spots or mottling.
- ☞ Wrap it up on the way home if the weather is cold.

☞ Check that the conditions in your home are suitable for the plant, that temperature and light are adequate.

Liven up limp pot plants by watering them daily with cold tea. The plants will benefit from the minerals in the tea.

Soak broken egg shells in a jar of water for a few days and then use the liquid to nourish your houseplants. You can also use the water left after boiling eggs for a similar effect (but cool it before use). Geraniums respond especially well to this.

Rotate all your pot plants each week to encourage them to grow straight. Plants naturally lean towards the light and if not turned they will grow crooked.

Cacti look wonderful if they are dusted occasionally with a pastry brush.

Wipe dusty leaves with the inside of a banana skin, which will remove the dust and nourish the leaves. They can also be shined by wiping with a mixture (a 50–50 blend) of milk and water.

Line the bottom of plant pots with paper coffee filters to stop soil leaking out.

Try growing your own houseplants from the leafy top of a pineapple or carrot. Once you have eaten the bits you want, plant the top in some compost and when it has started to grow, cover with a clear plastic bag secured with an elastic band to speed things up. Keep well watered and remove the bag when it looks established.

If you cannot arrange for a neighbor to water your houseplants while you are away on holiday, put an old towel in the bathtub and run two inches of cold water into the bath. Having ascertained that the pot drainage holes are large enough, put the plant pots on the towel and they will be able to take up water when they need it.

TRICKS OF THE TRADE

Do you ever find yourself running between the house and the garden to answer the phone for example? And how often do you give up the struggle with removing your rubber boots and just tramp mud inside? Keep a couple of old shower hats by the back door and slip them over your muddy shoes before you enter the house.

Avoid mosquito bites by rubbing exposed limbs with a few mint leaves. The aroma will also deter flies.

Label every plant you grow with a plastic label and indelible ink. When it is a mature two-year-old, and someone asks you what it is, you won't be embarrassed by a memory lapse! Cut up old plastic margarine tubs and use them.

As a general rule, don't buy cut flowers on a Monday, as they will have been left over from Saturday's delivery. Check that the stems look fresh below the waterline—any that appear slimy have probably spent a long time in the shop.

If your own garden cannot produce enough grass or plant cuttings to make your own mulch, try approaching your local park service or forestry commission administration. They usually have plenty to spare and it may be free or at least reasonably cheap.

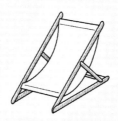

PETS

Prospective owners should take the time to research and familiarize themselves with the needs of the type of dog or cat they intend to keep. A cuddly, cute puppy may grow to a huge 80lb (30kg) dog that needs essential grooming and exercise daily. Cats, although having a reputation for independence, will need companionship and cannot be left for too long on their own. This section merely covers the tip of the iceberg when it comes to pet care, but it does provide a few handy hints. You cannot beat the advice of your local vet or other dog or cat owners if ever you are unsure.

A NEW DOG

In the early days reinforce the behavior you want from your new puppy. Other than safety issues it's best to generally ignore bad behavior and reward good.

When you leave a young puppy alone, give it one of your old T-shirts and leave a radio on. The dog will appreciate your smell, and the noise of the radio will replicate the sounds of a busy household.

Make the puppy a bed in a safe area and if he cries check up on him once to make sure nothing is wrong, but it is best to try and leave him after that rather than running to him at every sound so that he learns he can't demand constant attention.

Ensure that wires, plugs, and small things that could be choked on are well out of a little puppy's way—you will be surprised at the speed and the damage a pup can do in minutes.

Put a collar on the pup only when you are with him, but let him wear it a few hours a day before you try out walking on a lead. Walk early in the day or late at night in the hot weather.

A DOG'S BABY BLUES

Before a new baby arrives, begin to prepare your family dog. It is important that your dog associates the new baby with as few disruptions as possible and does not feel neglected.

If the dog is to be excluded from any room, make this a rule before the baby arrives home.

Reward the dog with treats for positive behavior around a baby.

Never leave any baby or child unattended with any dog.

A NEW CAT

For the first few days put the cat in a room that can be closed off from the rest of the house. Put the litter box and food on opposite sides of the room. Cats will not eat next to their litter box.

Give a new cat plenty of time to get used to their new home. Spend time with them so that they gain confidence and feel comfortable in their new surroundings.

Cats have a reputation for independence, but they do get lonely if they're alone for long stretches of time.

If your cat shies away from hard food, she may have a problem with her mouth or teeth. Check with your vet.

A cat will often knead against a favorite spot when she is content. This stems from kittenhood, when kittens knead against their mother to stimulate the flow of milk.

SERVING FOOD

Sprinkle baking soda around the outside of pet dishes to keep insects away from the pet food.

A teaspoon of olive oil on your pet's food every day will give your pet a glossy coat of fur and help to stop dry skin itching.

If your dog is recovering from an upset stomach, feed nothing more than water and plain boiled rice for 24 hours to allow his digestion to recover.

If your dog has an upset stomach, boil some rice and add it as a supplement to his or her food.

Dry eggshells and crush them very finely. Add them to cat and dog food as a mineral supplement.

KEEPING CLEAN

The best way to bath a cat is to find an old mesh window screen, place it in the tub or sink, the cat will dig its claws into the screen and stay there the entire time of bathing.

To remove pet hair from upholstery, use a damp sponge, or rub over with sticky tape, which will pick up the fur very effectively.

Use cooking oil to remove fresh paint from a pet's fur.

Crush burrs with pliers before combing out of your pet's hair. This makes removal much easier.

Spray the bottoms of your dog's feet with nonstick vegetable spray, and the snow won't get packed between the pads. The vegetable spray won't track onto the floor, either.

To fight fleas indoors, mix up several drops of oil of rosemary, penny-royal, or citronella with baking soda and sprinkle on the carpet, then vacuum up.

To remove pet urine, sop up as much moisture as possible with paper towels. Blot (don't rub) the spot with a mixture of one teaspoon of non-alkaline detergent per half pint (250ml) of lukewarm water, working from the outside to the inside of the area. Rinse with clear tap water.

To remove pet odor, blot the spot with a mixture of a third of a cup white wine vinegar in two-thirds of a cup warm water, and sprinkle with baking soda. Cover with half an inch (1cm) layer of paper towels weighted down by a heavy book and leave to dry.

If you want to keep pets off the furniture (and you have no small children), tuck mothballs under the seat cushions.

BIBLIOGRAPHY

Australian Women's Weekly, *The Household Manual: Essential Hints and Handy Tips,* 1990.

Beeton, Isabella, *The Book of Household Management,* 1861.

Bremner, Moyra, *Supertips,* Treasure Press, 1986.

Costantino, Maria, *Complete Household Hints,* D&S Books, 2003.

Digby, Helen, *The Dog Care Handbook,* D&S Books 2003.

Don, Montagu, *The Weekend Gardener,* Bloomsbury Publishing 1995.

Kent, Cassandra *Which? Way to Clean It,* Which Ltd., 1994.

Lapworth, Katherine and Fraser, Alexandra, *Trade Secrets,* Orion Media, 1998.

Lawson, Nigella, *How to Eat,* Chatto and Windus, 1998.

Wiseman, John 'Lofty', *The SAS Urban Survival Handbook* HarperCollins 1991.

Quigg, Mary Rose, *Mary Rose's 1001 Country Household Hints.*

Wardington, Lady, *Supertips for Life,* Michael Joseph, 1997.

Woodburn, Kim & MacKenzie, Aggie, *How Clean is your House?,* Michael Joseph, 2003.

WEBSITES

There are thousands of websites packed full of good ideas; this is just a tiny selection.

www.free-beauty-tips.com

www.gutenberg.net

www.greenhome.com

www.hints-n-tips.com

www.laundry-alternative.com

www.nsc.org

www.pagewise.com

www.redcross.org

www.rospa.org

www.tipking.com

www.virtuowl.com

www.wackyuses.com

www.101beautysecrets.com

Acknowledgments

Thanks to the following for generously sharing books, ideas and tips: Terry Atkins, Julie Blunden, Norna Exton, Clare Haworth-Maden, John Kitchen, Katie Kitchen, Eleanor Stillwell, Sheila Stockton, Catherine Woodehouse.

INDEX